EUROPEAN ROYALTY

OF THE

VICTORIAN AND EDWARDIAN ERA

EUROPEAN ROYALTY

OF THE

VICTORIAN AND EDWARDIAN ERA

JOHN FABB

Seaby

LONDON

B.A. Seaby Ltd
8 Cavendish Square
London W1M 0AJ

Distributed by
B.T. Batsford Ltd
P.O. Box 4, Braintree, Essex CM7 7QY

Printed and bound in Great Britain
by Butler & Tanner Ltd, Frome, Somerset

ISBN 0 900 652 91 8

CONTENTS

INTRODUCTION

A monarch once said that one day there would only be five Kings left in the world – the King of Clubs, the King of Hearts, the King of Diamonds, the King of Spades and the King of England. The change from absolute to constitutional monarchy in the mid nineteenth century was a blow to the royal houses, used to unquestioning acceptance of their divine right to rule.

It was at this time that photographs of Kings and Queens were first available to their people. Hitherto, monarchs had been known by their portraits or the image on their coins, or identified by the guards that surrounded them or the uniforms they wore. Only their intimate circle knew what they really looked like; ordinary people could only watch from afar as a carriage passed or a review took place. Photographs changed all that, and the real face of the monarch became well known, even to country folk. Kings and queens were seen to be just as ugly or handsome, fat or thin as their subjects. This lessened the aura of majesty, but benefitted posterity, as photographs captured many of the main historical figures of the previous century. It is fascinating to see the face of Queen Victoria's mother who married a brother of George IV, or that of King Ludwig of Bavaria, a godson of the ill-fated Queen Marie Antoinette of France. Family likenesses can be traced, or speculated about, as in the case of Napoleon I, who died before photography was invented, but whose illegitimate son Count Colonna Walewski is believed to be a close likeness of his illustrious father.

A King in ordinary clothes does not cut the dash of a romantic historical monarch, particularly in the mid nineteenth century, when clothes were very dull indeed, especially for men. Only a few were able to rise above this and be elegant and fashionable, but Edward VII of Great Britain and the Duke of Morny of France were always exceptionally well turned out. Military uniform often saved the day for the gentlemen, as many of the photographs show. This also has the advantage that the people could easily recognise their sovereign in a uniform, which proved a good second best to the full regalia of crown and robes. It was easier for the ladies to look fashionable, with the aid of the latest Paris creations. Queen Victoria was never dressed in the latest style, but as she was frequently pregnant during her married life, this was not entirely her fault. A contrast is provided by the photographs of the Grand Duchess Alice of Hesse and By Rhine and the dashing Queen Wilhelmina of the Netherlands.

The royal sideboards, like those of the common people, groaned under increasing collections of group photographs. Photographs were passed from one royal house to another to commemorate a marriage or the birth of a child. Queen Victoria in particular was an enthusiastic collector of photographs of her great family of Europe. She was connected to almost every great house by the marriages of her sons and daughters, and her royal connections increased with the birth of grandchildren, great-grandchildren and even great-great-grandchildren. Other royal families also collected photographs, to remind them of their children far away in foreign countries, as travel was difficult in those days, and affairs of state often prevented family reunions. Monarchs were much more closely involved in government than they are today, and many kings and queens put in long hours at the desk. Tsar Nikolai II, Emperor Franz Josef and Queen Victoria were particularly noted for their hard work.

It was also necessary to read the newspapers of the left and the right to keep abreast of what the people were thinking and not to rely completely on ministers, which had cost a throne or two in the past. There were also ceremonies to attend, in public and private. Only occasionally could the royal family escape from the gaze of the people to their hunting lodges or private yachts.

Life was not a bed of roses in every country, and on

occasion violence broke out. In the period covered by this book, a Tsar of Russia was blown up, a King of Portugal was shot, and so was a King of Serbia, and an Empress of Austria was stabbed. Six attempts on the life of Queen Victoria were made during her reign. For all that, most royal deaths were from causes that struck down ordinary folk during the Victorian era, such as heart attacks, pneumonia, typhoid, cancer, and just old age. Many monarchs, such as Queen Victoria and Emperor Franz Josef of Austria, as well as the later Kings of Sweden, lived to a great age. However, some were cut off in their prime. Great Britain lost the heir to the throne when Albert Victor, Duke of Clarence and Avondale, died of pneumonia at the age of twenty-eight. Crown Prince Rudolf of Austria shot himself at the age of thirty-one, and the Prince Imperial of France, the great hope of the Bonaparte cause, died in the Zulu War at the age of twenty-three.

Republics were virtually unheard of (except in France) and monarchies were at the height of their popularity. When Greece became independent from Turkey, it became a monarchy, and this path was followed by Bulgaria and Roumania when they too obtained independence. To carry on the tradition of hereditary monarchy, marriage was of prime importance. Monarchs needed to marry to consolidate their position, or to form an alliance with other great houses. Love often did find a way and the majority of couples were as happy and contented as any Victorian could expect to be. Families were large to ensure the succession, as death struck down Royalty and commoners alike. Queen Victoria had a large family; the Grand Duke Guillaume IV of Luxembourg had six daughters and yet no son to succeed; Tsar Nikolai II of Russia had four daughters before his son Alexis was born. Dynasties often came close to dying out when the direct line of succession failed; Queen Victoria herself was the only child born to the elderly Duke of Kent late in life. This situation was repeated in the Netherlands when King Willem's sons, as well as his wife, died before him. He married again, and his second wife gave him the heir to continue the House of Orange. King Alfonso XIII succeeded to the throne of Spain before he was born. Where nature failed entirely, politicians then stepped in to appoint an heir to put the matter right, as in Denmark on the death of King Carl XIII.

The photographs end just before 1914, when the First World War began. It ended with the collapse of the majority of the European dynasties. Before the war, thirty-nine countries had been ruled by hereditary families. In Germany alone, seventeen princes and four kings had lost their thrones by the end of the war. Royalty faded into the background, and modern and uninteresting politicians elbowed their way into the vacated limelight.

ACKNOWLEDGEMENTS

The author and publishers would like to thank the following for permission to reproduce copyright photographs:

BBC Hulton Picture Library   1, 4, 9, 12, 13, 17-19, 21-23, 47, 50, 52, 59, 70, 71, 78, 81, 83, 84, 89, 92, 101.

B.T. Batsford Limited   25, 27, 28, 31-36, 38, 40, 41, 43-46, 67.

Buffalo Bill Historical Centre, Cody, Wyoming   82.

The National Army Museum   6, 30.

National Portrait Gallery   29.

National Galleries of Scotland   24.

Royal Archives, The Hague   54-58, 72.

By gracious permission of Her Majesty the Queen   2, 3, 5, 7, 10, 11, 15, 16, 26, 48, 49, 51, 53, 60, 63, 65, 73-77, 79, 80, 86, 90, 91, 93, 94-98, 100, 102.

Victoria and Albert Museum   20, 39, 64, 85.

Illustrations   8, 14, 37, 42, 66, 68, 69, 87, 88 are from the author's collection.

Note

The family trees have been simplified. The dates given are those of birth, marriage and death. Names in capitals are those of monarchs and names in bold type are those who appear in the photographs that follow.

AUSTRIA

From 1848 to 1914, Austria was ruled by one man – Emperor Franz Josef, who succeeded to the throne at eighteen on the abdication of his uncle Ferdinand, who lived on until 1875. The original desk-bound monarch and a true civil servant, he outlived Queen Victoria by fifteen years. He regularly rose at 4 a.m. and worked until breakfast; lunch was served at midday and dinner at five. His routine was inflexible. There was an amusing clash with the King of England, Edward VII, when he visted the old Emperor. The court officials had great difficulty in bringing the two monarchs together, as the Emperor rose at 4 a.m., whereas King Edward did not even have coffee until 10 a.m., and although the King had to conform to the Emperor's meal times, he was quite unable to go to bed at 7.30 p.m., when the Emperor normally retired. Franz Josef's passion was his army,

and he was never out of uniform, as can be seen from the photographs. Every year he attended military manoeuvres.

His private life was unhappy, with the assassination of his Empress, Elisabeth of Bavaria in 1898. Their only son, Crown Prince Rudolf, shot himself and his mistress at Mayerling in 1889. His brother, the Emperor Maximilian of Mexico, was shot by a firing squad, his sister-in-law, the Empress of Mexico, went mad, and finally his nephew and heir, Grand Duke Franz Ferdinand was murdered together with his wife at Sarajevo, which precipitated the First World War.

Although outside the scope of this book, the old Emperor was succeeded in 1916 by his great-nephew Archduke Karl, who was only twenty-seven, and who immediately began peace proceedings with the Allies, but his attempts unfortunately failed.

AUSTRIA and HUNGARY

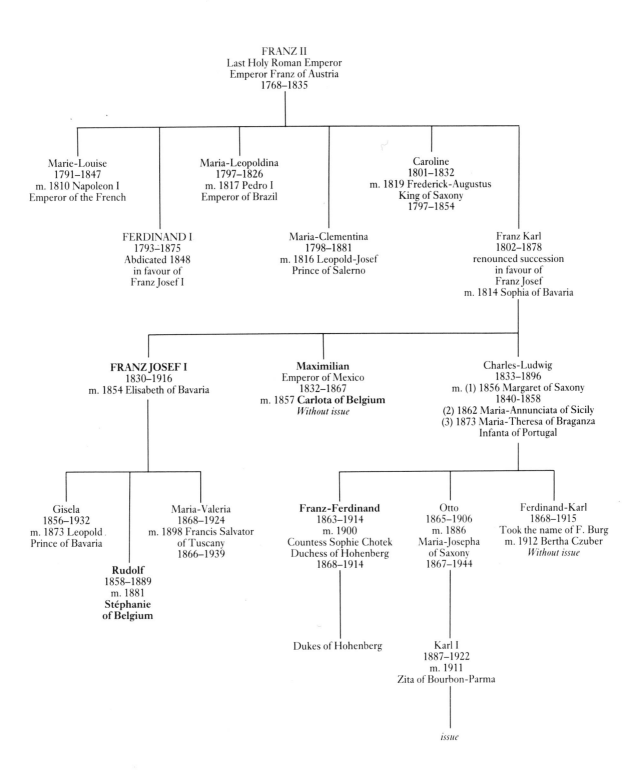

FRANZ II
Last Holy Roman Emperor
Emperor Franz of Austria
1768–1835

Marie-Louise
1791–1847
m. 1810 Napoleon I
Emperor of the French

Maria-Leopoldina
1797–1826
m. 1817 Pedro I
Emperor of Brazil

Caroline
1801–1832
m. 1819 Frederick-Augustus
King of Saxony
1797–1854

FERDINAND I
1793–1875
Abdicated 1848
in favour of
Franz Josef I

Maria-Clementina
1798–1881
m. 1816 Leopold-Josef
Prince of Salerno

Franz Karl
1802–1878
renounced succession
in favour of
Franz Josef
m. 1814 Sophia of Bavaria

FRANZ JOSEF I
1830–1916
m. 1854 Elisabeth of Bavaria

Maximilian
Emperor of Mexico
1832–1867
m. 1857 **Carlota of Belgium**
Without issue

Charles-Ludwig
1833–1896
m. (1) 1856 Margaret of Saxony
1840-1858
(2) 1862 Maria-Annunciata of Sicily
(3) 1873 Maria-Theresa of Braganza
Infanta of Portugal

Gisela
1856–1932
m. 1873 Leopold
Prince of Bavaria

Maria-Valeria
1868–1924
m. 1898 Francis Salvator
of Tuscany
1866–1939

Franz-Ferdinand
1863–1914
m. 1900
Countess Sophie Chotek
Duchess of Hohenberg
1868–1914

Otto
1865–1906
m. 1886
Maria-Josepha
of Saxony
1867–1944

Ferdinand-Karl
1868–1915
Took the name of F. Burg
m. 1912 Bertha Czuber
Without issue

Rudolf
1858–1889
m. 1881
**Stéphanie
of Belgium**

Dukes of Hohenberg

Karl I
1887–1922
m. 1911
Zita of Bourbon-Parma

issue

1   Emperor Ferdinand I of Austria, King of Hungary and Bohemia (1793–1875)
Ferdinand succeeded to the throne in 1835. He was mentally deficient, and would have been passed over as Emperor, were it not for Franz II's insistence on the legitimate succession of his eldest son. He abdicated in 1848 in favour of his nephew, Franz Josef I, and lived in Prague until his death at the age of 82. His sister Marie Louise married Emperor Napoleon I of France in 1810.

2   *Right* Emperor Franz Josef I, Emperor of Austria, King of Hungary and Bohemia, with Crown Prince Rudolf, *c.* 1860
Franz Josef succeeded to the throne at the age of eighteen and reigned for sixty-eight years. His life, however, was filled with tragedy. His wife, the beautiful Empress Elisabeth, a hypersensitive and artistic Bavarian Princess, was stabbed to death by an Italian fanatic in 1898. Previously the Emperor's younger brother Maximilian had been shot in Mexico, and his only son, depicted in the photograph, had committed suicide. Finally, his nephew and heir, Archduke Franz Ferdinand, was murdered in 1914 at Sarajevo. The old Emperor died in 1916, as the Empire crumbled about him.

3 *Left* **Emperor Maximilian and Empress Carlota of Mexico, 1857**

Maximilian was the younger brother of the Austrian Emperor Franz Josef and formerly an Archduke of Austria. His wife was a Princess of Belgium. The French encouraged him to accept the throne of Mexico, but when the couple landed they found the country in chaos, with enormous debts, and a volatile political situation. There was also a conflict with the supporters of Benito Juarez, the late President of Mexico. French troops withdrew in 1865, and the civil war soon ended with the defeat of the Emperor. He was shot by a firing squad on the morning of 19 June 1867; the Empress lost her reason and remained insane for the rest of her life, dying in 1927.

4 Congress of the German Princes at Frankfurt on Main, August, 1863.

This was called to try and maintain Austria's dominant position over Germany and to contain the rising power of Prussia and the ambitions of Bismarck and Von Moltke. It failed, and in 1866 Prussia was at war with Austria. In the centre of the steps, in the white uniform, stands the Austrian Emperor Franz Josef. To the right of the Emperor stands King George of Hanover. On the left of the Emperor is King Maximilian of Bavaria; on King Maximilian's left is King John I of Saxony. Behind the Emperor, in civilian clothes, stands Prince Frederick of the Netherlands, representing the Grand Duchy of Luxembourg. At the top of the stairs on the left, in uniform, is Grand Duke Karl Alexander of Saxe-Weimar-Eisenach. On the extreme left in the front row is Ernest II, Duke of Saxe-Coburg-Gotha. The last figure on the extreme right is Crown Prince Karl of Württemburg. Next to him is Ludwig III, Grand Duke of Hesse and by Rhine. Fourth from the right is Adolphe, Duke of Nassau, and on his right, Friedrich I, Grand Duke of Baden.

5 *Left* **Crown Prince Rudolf and Crown Princess Stephanie of Austria, *c.* 1885**

The young Prince's successes with women were so numerous that it was hastily decided to marry him off to a suitable Catholic Princess. The prince was already blasé and bored. Having been horrified by several large German princesses, he was sent to Belgium, where King Leopold II arranged an alliance between his daughter and Prince Rudolf. Princess Stephanie was youthful, but had not the charms to keep Rudolf attentive to her. He soon slipped back to his bachelor habits, and Baroness Maria Vetsera. Depressed by his family and irritated that his father would not give him a positive role in the Empire, he shot himself and his mistress at Mayerling in 1889.

6 Grand Duke Franz Ferdinand at Hyderabad, India, 1893

The Grand Duke, seated second from right, was on an official visit to British India. He became heir presumptive to the throne of the Austrian Empire in 1889, after the death of Crown Prince Rudolf. His own death at Sarajevo in 1914 precipitated the First World War. Seated on the Grand Duke's left is his host, His Highness Sir Mahbub Ali Khan, Sixth Nizam of Hyderabad. At each end sit respectively the Grand Duke's aide and the British political officer. Behind the Nizam, in native dress, stands the commander of his personal bodyguard. The guards were volunteers from Africa, recruited and sent from that continent, and of the Moslem faith.

THE BALKANS

The Balkans consisted of six kingdoms, all of which had been part of the Turkish Empire.

When Greece became independent, the Great Powers decided that a monarchy would best unite the country. The throne was offered to Prince Otto of Bavaria, younger son of King Ludwig I of Bavaria. He accepted, but unfortunately insisted on bringing both Bavarian soldiers and administrators with him, and on keeping an expensive court. He failed to produce an heir, and a revolution broke out in 1843, when he granted a constitution, and so managed to retain the throne until a second revolution in 1862. He and his wife, Amelie of Oldenburg, then fled the country.

After the revolution a new king was chosen, Prince William of Denmark, who was proclaimed George I King of the Hellenes. It was a volatile country, but he managed to stay on his throne for fifty years. It was truly a lifetime spent in the service of his adopted country.

Roumania (now Rumania) was formed from the two principalities of Wallachia and Moldavia, and in 1866 the Parliament offered the throne to Prince Karl Eitel of Hohenzollern-Sigmaringen, a twenty-seven year old Prussian Army officer. He was crowned as Carol I at Bucharest in 1881, and reigned until 1914. Austere with a strong sense of duty, Carol I was able to weather the political storms and wars that raged in the later part of the nineteenth century.

Bulgaria was once part of the Turkish Empire, and became the Principality of Bulgaria in 1878. The first elected King was Prince Alexander of Battenberg, whose brother had married a daughter of Queen Victoria. His guarantor was Russia, who forced him off the throne by a coup when he began to exert a little independence. Although a counter revolution set him back on the throne, he abdicated a few days later. The Government then chose Prince Ferdinand of Saxe-Coburg-Gotha, a very clever and rich young man, who managed to retain his throne until he made the mistake in 1914 of backing the Germans in the First World War, and was forced to abdicate in favour of his son, Boris.

Serbia was also at one time part of the Turkish Empire, but had won independence early in the nineteenth century. It was ruled in the mid century by the Obrenovic family. Prince Michael, who ruled from 1859, was able to get the Turkish army to withdraw their garrisons from the country. He was an able and refined man, but unfortunately he was assassinated in 1868 by the rival family of Karageorgevic. Prince Michael was succeeded by his cousin Milan who was only fourteen. He was able to proclaim himself King of Serbia after the Russo-Turkish War of 1877. He also was a clever and able ruler, but with a weakness for beautiful women. His son Alexander became king at twelve years old and seized power from his regents when he was sixteen. Unfortunately his liaison with a widowed lady-in-waiting, Draga Mashin, whom he later married, led to their deaths at the hands of a party of army officers. The throne was then offered to the rival family of Karageorgevic in the person of Prince Peter in 1903.

Montenegro was the smallest state in the Balklans, and was recognised as an independent principality in 1878, after the Russo-Turkish war. Nikola I was the ruling prince at this time. He proclaimed himself king in 1910. Powerfully built and very tall, he always wore his national dress. His family had many marriage links with powerful European houses; his eldest daughter had married King Peter of Serbia, and another was Queen of Italy. Two of his daughters were Russian Grand Duchesses, and another was married to Prince Franz Josef of Battenberg.

Albania did not became a kingdom until 1913, at the end of the Balkan wars with Turkey. The throne was then offered to Prince Wilhelm of Wied, who arrived in 1914. The new King found insurrections, disturbances and intrigue. With the outbreak of the First World War, the throne became untenable, the subsidies due from France and Italy were no longer paid and so the King and his family left the country for Germany. King Wilhelm never returned and died in 1945.

GREECE

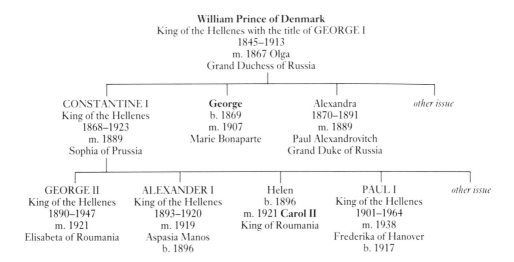

William Prince of Denmark
King of the Hellenes with the title of GEORGE I
1845–1913
m. 1867 Olga
Grand Duchess of Russia

CONSTANTINE I
King of the Hellenes
1868–1923
m. 1889
Sophia of Prussia

George
b. 1869
m. 1907
Marie Bonaparte

Alexandra
1870–1891
m. 1889
Paul Alexandrovitch
Grand Duke of Russia

other issue

GEORGE II
King of the Hellenes
1890–1947
m. 1921
Elisabeta of Roumania

ALEXANDER I
King of the Hellenes
1893–1920
m. 1919
Aspasia Manos
b. 1896

Helen
b. 1896
m. 1921 **Carol II**
King of Roumania

PAUL I
King of the Hellenes
1901–1964
m. 1938
Frederika of Hanover
b. 1917

other issue

ROUMANIA

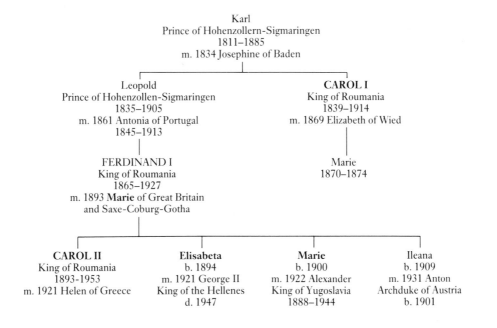

Karl
Prince of Hohenzollern-Sigmaringen
1811–1885
m. 1834 Josephine of Baden

Leopold
Prince of Hohenzollern-Sigmaringen
1835–1905
m. 1861 Antonia of Portugal
1845–1913

CAROL I
King of Roumania
1839–1914
m. 1869 Elizabeth of Wied

FERDINAND I
King of Roumania
1865–1927
m. 1893 **Marie** of Great Britain
and Saxe-Coburg-Gotha

Marie
1870–1874

CAROL II
King of Roumania
1893-1953
m. 1921 Helen of Greece

Elisabeta
b. 1894
m. 1921 George II
King of the Hellenes
d. 1947

Marie
b. 1900
m. 1922 Alexander
King of Yugoslavia
1888–1944

Ileana
b. 1909
m. 1931 Anton
Archduke of Austria
b. 1901

SERBIA

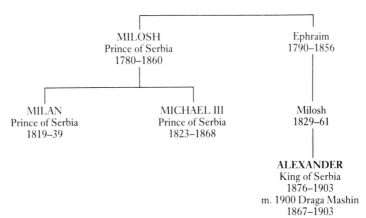

```
                    MILOSH                              Ephraim
                Prince of Serbia                       1790–1856
                   1780–1860
                                                           │
           ┌───────────────┴───────────────┐           Milosh
         MILAN                       MICHAEL III        1829–61
    Prince of Serbia               Prince of Serbia        │
       1819–39                        1823–1868        ALEXANDER
                                                       King of Serbia
                                                        1876–1903
                                                    m. 1900 Draga Mashin
                                                        1867–1903
```

MONTENEGRO

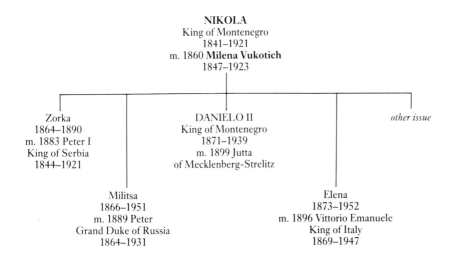

```
                         NIKOLA
                    King of Montenegro
                        1841–1921
                 m. 1860 Milena Vukotich
                        1847–1923

   ┌──────────────────────┬──────────────────────┐
 Zorka                  DANIELO II            other issue
1864–1890           King of Montenegro
m. 1883 Peter I        1871–1939
King of Serbia      m. 1899 Jutta
1844–1921        of Mecklenberg-Strelitz

        Militsa                    Elena
       1866–1951                 1873–1952
    m. 1889 Peter           m. 1896 Vittorio Emanuele
  Grand Duke of Russia         King of Italy
       1864–1931                 1869–1947
```

7 *Right* **Otto I, King of Greece, c. 1860**
Prince Otto of Bavaria, younger son of King Ludwig I of Bavaria, was chosen as king when Greece became independent in 1833. He made Greece fashionable for buildings and art decoration, but unfortunately brought both Bavarian troops and administrators with him. He also maintained a grand court which Greece could ill afford, and his unpopularity increased when he failed to produce an heir. A revolution broke out in 1843, but having granted a constitution and agreed to the departure of the Bavarian soldiers, King Otto ruled until a second revolution in 1862.

8 Prince George of Greece and torpedo officers of the Greek Navy, 1897
Prince George, the second son of King George I, is sitting in the centre of this group of officers. He became an admiral of the Greek Navy. In 1907 he married Princess Marie Bonaparte, the author of several books on psychoanalysis. Her father was Prince Roland Bonaparte, who had married the millionairess, Marie Blanc.

9 *Right* Frederick VIII of Denmark and his brother George I, of Greece, 1906
King Frederick and King George were both members of the Royal House of Denmark and sons of King Christian IX. Their sister was Queen Alexandra of Great Britain. George accepted the throne offered to him by the Greek National Assembly in 1863. He had no illusions about his chances of keeping the throne, and used to say that he 'kept a portmanteau ready packed'. However, he was to be King of Greece for fifty years.

10   Crown Princess Marie of Roumania with Prince Carol, Princess Elisabeta and Princess Marie, 1900

The Crown Princess was the daughter of Queen Victoria's second son Prince Alfred, Duke of Edinburgh. In 1893 she married Crown Prince Ferdinand of Roumania, who succeeded to the throne in 1914. On the left stands Prince Carol who became King in 1930. The baby is Princess Marie who was born that year, and who subsequently married King Alexander of Yugoslavia. The other little girl is Princess Elisabeta, who married King George II of Greece in 1921. The Crown Princess ran a cholera camp during the Balkan Wars and also found time to write fairy stories.

11   *Right* Carol I of Roumania, October 1888

Prince Karl Eitel of Hohenzollern-Sigmaringen, a twenty-seven year old Prussian army officer with the backing of Bismarck, was chosen by the state of Roumania as their king. This was in 1866 when Wallachia and Moldavia, who had achieved self government after the Crimean War, united into one state. The new King was energetic, hard-headed and a true Prussian. He ruled his country with a strong sense of duty; staunchly German in his sympathies, but also unscrupulous when the interests of his country demanded it. The crown which he placed on his own head at his coronation was made from captured Turkish guns. By the end of the nineteenth century Roumania was rich in coal and oil and had become the leading Balkan state.

12 *Above, opposite* **Kaiser Wilhelm II, King of Prussia and King Ferdinand of Bulgaria during the state visit to Berlin in 1907**
King Ferdinand was known as 'the fox'. A very clever man, and a brilliant and highly amusing conversationalist, he liked to be thought more of an intriguer than he actually was. He was also a very rich man and a collector of precious stones.

13 *Below, opposite* **Alexander, King of Serbia, c. 1900**
In 1900 Alexander married a widow named Draga Mashin, who was one of his mother's ladies-in-waiting. The marriage made him extremely unpopular, and nobody liked Draga as Queen either. In June 1903, troops surrounded the palace and a party of officers broke down the bedroom door of the King and Queen. Finding them hiding in a secret

room, they shot them down, and threw the bodies out of the window into the garden below. The throne was then offered to the rival family dynasty of Karageorgevic, and Peter I was proclaimed.

14 *Above* **The Prince and Princess of Montenegro, and suite, c. 1900**
Nikola I, Prince of Montenegro, ruled this small mountainous state for sixty years, from 1860 to 1918. He assumed the title of King in 1910. The strategic position of Montenegro in the Balkans gave the King political power amongst the European nations, and he made strong alliances by marriage. His eldest son married Princess Jutta of Mecklenburg-Strelitz. His daughter Elena married the King of Italy, and the others married Russian Grand Dukes. Although Montenegro troops fought for the Allies in the First World War, they were defeated by Serbia and became part of the kingdom of Yugoslavia.

FrancE

Royal and imperiaL

In 1848 Louis-Philippe, King of France had lost his throne, and a Republic was established once more. However, the French elected as President, Napoleon, son of Louis King of Holland and brother of Emperor Napoleon I. Four years later he proclaimed himself Emperor Napoleon III. In 1853 he married the beautiful Eugénie de Montijo, daughter of the Count of Montijo, and three years later they had a son, the Prince Imperial. The Eagle soared with the victory in the Crimea, the Austrian defeat in Italy and the expansion of an overseas empire. However, by the 1860's corruption had set in, and the Eagle fell still further after the withdrawal of French support to the Mexican Empire which had been set up by France. This ended in the death of the Emperor Maximilian of Mexico at the hand of the insurgents. Drawn into a war with Germany in 1870, France was quickly and soundly defeated by the well-oiled German fighting machine, just as Chancellor Bismarck planned. The Emperor Napoleon was himself captured at the Battle of Sedan, after seeking death in vain on the battlefield. The Imperial Family retired to England where the Emperor died in 1873. The Empress Eugénie, a tragic figure, lived on until 1920 when she died at the great age of ninety-four.

The Royal House of France kept a low profile during this period, as there were no vibrant figures with dynamic personalities to lead their cause. Henri Duc de Bordeaux, the last of the legitimate line, died in 1883. The move to restore the monarchy after the fall of the Empire came to nothing, although the family of Louis-Philippe were then regarded as the rightful heirs to the throne of France. In 1886 the royal family were obliged to leave France when the Third Republic passed its law of exile. They moved to England and settled at Stowe, the vast palace built by the Dukes of Buckingham.

FRANCE: ROYAL

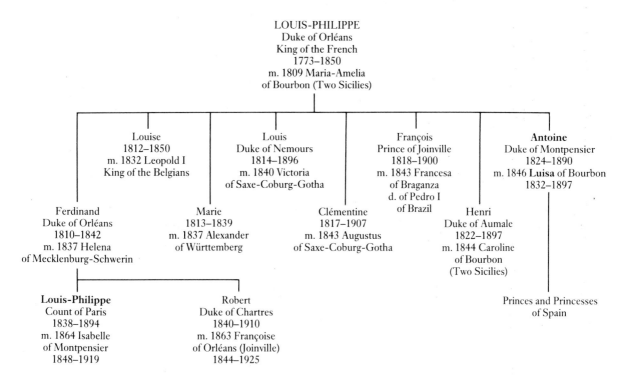

LOUIS-PHILIPPE
Duke of Orléans
King of the French
1773–1850
m. 1809 Maria-Amelia
of Bourbon (Two Sicilies)

Louise
1812–1850
m. 1832 Leopold I
King of the Belgians

Louis
Duke of Nemours
1814–1896
m. 1840 Victoria
of Saxe-Coburg-Gotha

François
Prince of Joinville
1818–1900
m. 1843 Francesa
of Braganza
d. of Pedro I
of Brazil

Antoine
Duke of Montpensier
1824–1890
m. 1846 **Luisa** of Bourbon
1832–1897

Ferdinand
Duke of Orléans
1810–1842
m. 1837 Helena
of Mecklenburg-Schwerin

Marie
1813–1839
m. 1837 Alexander
of Württemberg

Clémentine
1817–1907
m. 1843 Augustus
of Saxe-Coburg-Gotha

Henri
Duke of Aumale
1822–1897
m. 1844 Caroline
of Bourbon
(Two Sicilies)

Louis-Philippe
Count of Paris
1838–1894
m. 1864 Isabelle
of Montpensier
1848–1919

Robert
Duke of Chartres
1840–1910
m. 1863 Françoise
of Orléans (Joinville)
1844–1925

Princes and Princesses
of Spain

FRANCE: IMPERIAL

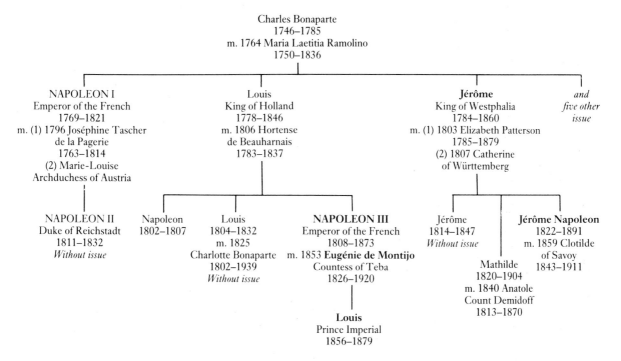

Charles Bonaparte
1746–1785
m. 1764 Maria Laetitia Ramolino
1750–1836

NAPOLEON I
Emperor of the French
1769–1821
m. (1) 1796 Joséphine Tascher
de la Pagerie
1763–1814
(2) Marie-Louise
Archduchess of Austria

Louis
King of Holland
1778–1846
m. 1806 Hortense
de Beauharnais
1783–1837

Jérôme
King of Westphalia
1784–1860
m. (1) 1803 Elizabeth Patterson
1785–1879
(2) 1807 Catherine
of Württemberg

*and
five other
issue*

NAPOLEON II
Duke of Reichstadt
1811–1832
Without issue

Napoleon
1802–1807

Louis
1804–1832
m. 1825
Charlotte Bonaparte
1802–1939
Without issue

NAPOLEON III
Emperor of the French
1808–1873
m. 1853 **Eugénie de Montijo**
Countess of Teba
1826–1920

Jérôme
1814–1847
Without issue

Jérôme Napoleon
1822–1891
m. 1859 Clotilde
of Savoy
1843–1911

Mathilde
1820–1904
m. 1840 Anatole
Count Demidoff
1813–1870

Louis
Prince Imperial
1856–1879

15 Prince Antoine, Duke of Montpensier, c. 1860.

The youngest son of King Louis-Philippe of France, he married the Infanta Luisa Ferdinanda of Spain, younger sister of Queen Isabella II. He had hoped to wrest the crown from Isabella and have himself proclaimed King of Spain. He spent a sizeable fortune to that end, but without success. The daughter in the photograph is Princess Maria Isabella who married Louis-Philippe, Count of Paris and head of the Royal House of France. His younger daughter Maria married King Alfonso XII of Spain and so reconciled the two branches of the family. Unfortunately the new Queen died six months later.

16 *Right* Louis-Philippe, Count of Paris, 1858

He succeeded his grandfather, King Louis-Philippe I, as head of the House of Orleans, and was regarded by the legitimists as Philippe VII, King of France and Navarre. He married his cousin Maria Isabella, the Infanta of Spain. They settled in England during the Second Empire and waited impatiently for the opportunity to return to France. When the Empire fell, all the Princes immediately returned to France and offered to place their swords at the service of their country. They were politely conducted back to the frontier, although later their estates and property were returned to them.

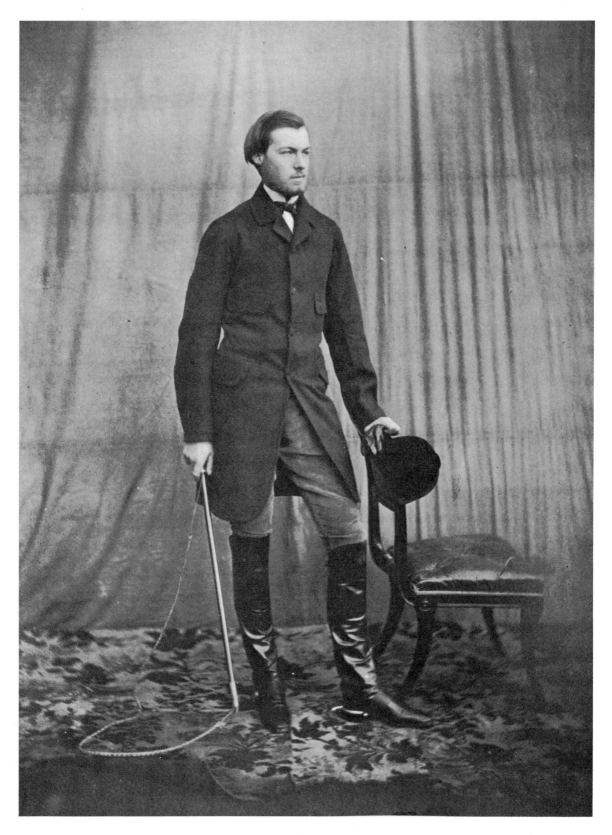

17 Emperor Napoleon III watching his son the Prince Imperial about to be photographed, 1858
The prince is two years old in this picture. At the age of three he attended his first military review, on his own pony. Raised on tales of *La Grande Armée*, encouraged to look upon soldiering as the only worthwhile profession, and surrounded all day by gorgeously uniformed soldiers, he became increasingly conscious of the name he bore. He was only six when he visited the great military camp at Chalon, and when asked to propose a toast, answered "A l'armée". At the fall of the Second Empire in 1870 he came to England and joined the British Army. He was reluctantly allowed to go to the Zulu War in 1879, where he died tragically in a small skirmish far from home. This was a terrible blow to the Bonapartists' cause.

18 *Right* Empress Eugénie of France, 1870
The daughter of the Spanish Count of Montijo, who had served the first Napoleon with much distinction and bravery. Napoleon III was introduced to the young Countess while inspecting his army at Satory, and was charmed by her beauty and horsemanship. After their marriage the Empress united the Napoleonic relatives in their hatred of her, which lasted throughout her life. Cold and aloof, she soon extinguished the ardour of Napoleon III. After the birth of their only child the Prince Imperial, he found consolation in the arms of his many mistresses. The Empress lived on to witness the fall of the Empire in 1870, the death of the Emperor in 1873 and, the final shattering blow, the death of the Prince Imperial in 1879. Eugénie died in 1920 at the age of ninety-six. The jewels that the Empress is wearing were auctioned off at the end of the Empire and were bought by the Maharajah of Patiala.

19 *Above, left* **Jerome, King of Westphalia, 1857**
Surviving brother of Napoleon I, Emperor of France, and the only one to be photographed. His kingdom was carved out of Western Germany by the Emperor and was lost in the defeat of 1815. He was a frivolous spendthrift, with none of the attributes of his brother the Emperor. He was married three times, first to Elizabeth Patterson of Baltimore, U.S.A.; secondly to Catherine, Princess of Württemburg, and thirdly to the Marchesa Bartolini-Baldelli. The last link with the First Empire, he died in 1860, at the age of seventy-five, at the zenith of the Second Empire. A gallant old roué, at military parades in his marshal's uniform he was said to look remarkably like Napoleon I.

20 *Above, right* **Prince Napoleon Bonaparte, 1860.**
The ill-natured and bad-tempered son of King Jerome of Westphalia, he wears the uniform of a General of Division. He had been sent out to the Crimea, where his record was singularly unspectacular. At thirty-seven he married Princess

Clotilde of Savoy, a plain girl with a considerable dowry. Unfortunately his marriage did not lead him to give up his mistresses, the most notable of whom were Rachel the actress and Cora Pearl. On the death of the Prince Imperial in 1879, he became head of the Imperial House. He died in exile in Rome in 1891.

21 *Opposite* **Alexander, Count Colonna-Walewski, 1860.**
The natural son of Emperor Napoleon I of France and the Polish patriot Countess Marie Walewski. Honest, urbane and incorruptible, he inherited little from his father except his looks. He became French Ambassador to England and a senator, and his first wife was Caroline Montague, daughter of the Earl of Sandwich. After her death he kept a mistress, the celebrated tragedienne Rachel, who bore him a son. The affair ended when on paying her an unexpected call one evening, he met the Duc de Gramont just leaving. His second wife was Marie Anne de Ricci, a member of the illustrious Polish family of Poniatowski and a beauty of the Second Empire.

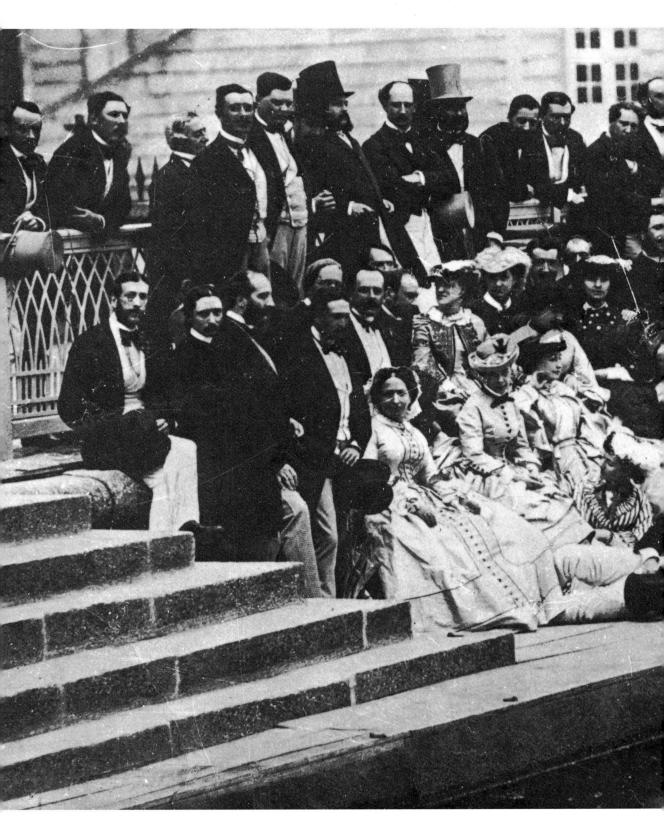

22 The French Imperial Court at Fontainebleau, 1860
Empress Eugénie sits with her ladies-in-waiting. She is the third from left, with her hand raised. Emperor Napoleon and the Prince Imperial sit in the boat. On the extreme right, wearing a top hat, stands Prince Metternich Winneburg, the famous statesman. The gentleman fifth from the left, standing at the back, is Count Colonna Walewski, natural son of Napoleon I.

38

23 *Left* **Charles, Duc de Morny, 1850**
He was half-brother of Emperor Napoleon III. Their
mother was Hortense de Beauharnais, daughter of
Napoleon I's wife the Empress Josephine by her first
marriage. Hortense married Napoleon's younger
brother Louis, created King of Holland, and their son
was Napoleon III. However, an affair with a French
General, Charles de Flahaut, resulted in the birth of
a son, Charles, Duc de Morny. A man of the Second
Empire, superbly tailored, he was to be seen
everywhere in smart society. On the doors of his
carriages was his escutcheon, bearing a hydrangea
(Hortensia) with a bar sinister, the sign of illegitimacy.
He became Ambassador to Russia and married
Princess Sophie Troubetskoi, a lady-in-waiting to
the Tsarina. He also kept for a while as his mistress
the notable Cora Pearl, who once had herself served
up on a silver salver, borne by four footmen. She was
naked, but decorated with a little parsley. As de
Morny lay dying in 1865, his friend the Marquis de
Montguyon flushed his love letters down the lavatory.
The Duc's famous collection of pornographic
photographs disappeared at the same time.

24   Charles Sobieski Stuart, *c*. 1840
Charles and his brother John claimed to be the
descendents of Bonnie Prince Charlie and heirs to
the throne of the United Kingdom. They fought for
Napoleon I, and were with him at the battles of
Dresden, Leipzig and Waterloo. In London they
learnt Gaelic, and then moved to Edinburgh about
1818. Later they lived in Argyllshire, and in 1845 they
moved to Prague in Bohemia, where they were
treated as royalty. In 1868 they were back in London.
Many prominent people of the time supported their
claim but there has never been absolute proof that
they were scions of the House of Stuart.

GREAT BRITAIN

The whole of this period was dominated by Queen Victoria who reigned from 1837 until 1901. The Queen was only eighteen when she was crowned, and her long reign restored the reputation of the monarchy, which had been tarnished in the eyes of the people by the two previous kings and their brothers, with their numerous mistresses and liaisons. Her marriage to Prince Albert of Saxe-Coburg-Gotha was a success beyond all expectations. Prince Albert was a serious and hard-working husband, and his premature death in 1861 was a blow from which the queen never recovered. Their nine children connected Great Britain to every court of Europe by their marriages, and Queen Victoria became the Grandmother of Europe. Her eldest daughter Victoria became Empress of Germany; Princess Alice, Grand Duchess of Hesse and by Rhine; Princess Helena, Princess of Schleswig-Holstein. Victoria's second son succeeded his uncle as Duke of Saxe-Coburg-Gotha, and her eldest son, who succeeded as Edward VII, married Alexandra Princess of Denmark, whose sister was Tsarina of All The Russias. The family of Queen Victoria continued to grow throughout her sixty years as Queen and Empress.

King Edward VII was fifty-nine when he succeeded his mother in 1901. A more cosmopolitan ruler and an esteemed diplomat, he was also a leader of society who enjoyed the company of beautiful women. His short reign ended on his death in 1910. He was in turn succeeded by his eldest surviving son George V who was forty-four. A very different man from his father, he preferred family life to society, but had a strong feeling for kingship, and was even crowned Emperor of India in a magnificent ceremony at Delhi. This was the highwater mark of Empire before the beginning of the First World War three years later.

GREAT BRITAIN

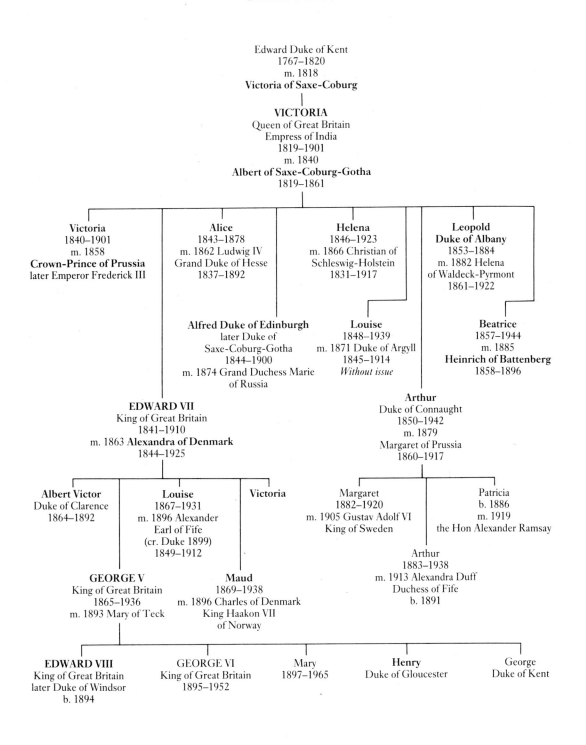

Edward Duke of Kent
1767–1820
m. 1818
Victoria of Saxe-Coburg

VICTORIA
Queen of Great Britain
Empress of India
1819–1901
m. 1840
Albert of Saxe-Coburg-Gotha
1819–1861

Victoria
1840–1901
m. 1858
Crown-Prince of Prussia
later Emperor Frederick III

Alice
1843–1878
m. 1862 Ludwig IV
Grand Duke of Hesse
1837–1892

Helena
1846–1923
m. 1866 Christian of
Schleswig-Holstein
1831–1917

Leopold
Duke of Albany
1853–1884
m. 1882 Helena
of Waldeck-Pyrmont
1861–1922

Alfred Duke of Edinburgh
later Duke of
Saxe-Coburg-Gotha
1844–1900
m. 1874 Grand Duchess Marie
of Russia

Louise
1848–1939
m. 1871 Duke of Argyll
1845–1914
Without issue

Beatrice
1857–1944
m. 1885
Heinrich of Battenberg
1858–1896

Arthur
Duke of Connaught
1850–1942
m. 1879
Margaret of Prussia
1860–1917

EDWARD VII
King of Great Britain
1841–1910
m. 1863 **Alexandra of Denmark**
1844–1925

Albert Victor
Duke of Clarence
1864–1892

Louise
1867–1931
m. 1896 Alexander
Earl of Fife
(cr. Duke 1899)
1849–1912

Victoria

Margaret
1882–1920
m. 1905 Gustav Adolf VI
King of Sweden

Patricia
b. 1886
m. 1919
the Hon Alexander Ramsay

GEORGE V
King of Great Britain
1865–1936
m. 1893 Mary of Teck

Maud
1869–1938
m. 1896 Charles of Denmark
King Haakon VII
of Norway

Arthur
1883–1938
m. 1913 Alexandra Duff
Duchess of Fife
b. 1891

EDWARD VIII
King of Great Britain
later Duke of Windsor
b. 1894

GEORGE VI
King of Great Britain
1895–1952

Mary
1897–1965

Henry
Duke of Gloucester

George
Duke of Kent

25 Queen Victoria and Prince Albert in 1854
An early photograph of the royal couple. The Queen
was thirty-five at the time, and Prince Albert was
three months older. They had married in 1840 and
were to have four sons and five daughters by the time
Prince Albert died in 1861. Prince Albert was the
younger son of Ernest I, Duke of Saxe-Coburg-
Gotha.

**26 *Right* Prince Alfred with the Duchess of
Kent, *c.* 1859**
The Duchess of Kent was the mother of Queen
Victoria. She was born Victoria, Princess of Saxe-
Coburg-Saafeld, and first married Erich Karl, Prince
of Leiningen. In 1818, she married Edward Duke of
Kent, son of George III.

  Prince Alfred was the second son of Queen
Victoria. He was born in 1844, created Duke of
Edinburgh in 1866, and succeeded his uncle to the
Dukedom of Saxe-Coburg-Gotha in 1893. He also
became an Admiral of the Fleet, an Admiral of the
Imperial German Navy and a General of the Prussian
Army, before his death in 1900.

27 Queen Victoria and Prince Albert with their children on the terrace at Osborne, soon after the birth of Princess Beatrice in 1857
Standing next to Prince Albert is Prince Alfred. From left to right are Princess Helena who married Prince Friedrich Christian of Schleswig-Holstein, Princess Alice who married Ludwig IV, Grand Duke of Hesse and by Rhine, and Prince Arthur, Duke of Connaught and Strathearn, in Highland dress. The Queen holds baby Beatrice, who married Prince Heinrich of Battenberg. Standing behind the Queen is her eldest daughter Victoria, the Princess Royal, who married Friedrich III, Emperor of Germany and King of Prussia. In front of the Princess Royal is Princess Louise, who married John Campbell, Ninth Duke of Argyll. Also at the front is Prince Leopold, Duke of Albany. On the extreme right stands Edward, Prince of Wales, later Edward VII.

28 *Above* **Queen Victoria out for a drive,** *c.* **1880**
The carriage is drawn up outside Balmoral Castle. Sitting beside the Queen is Princess Beatrice, her youngest daughter and constant companion after the death of Prince Albert in 1861. On the box next to the coachman is Queen Victoria's servant John Brown, generally disliked by the royal family and the servants. He died in 1883, from a chill caught searching the grounds for intruders. Some say he fell over drunk in the grounds, lay there all night and thus caught a chill.

29 *Right* **Prince Arthur, Duke of Connaught and Strathearn, 1857**
The prince was the third son of Queen Victoria. Dressed in the uniform of a drummer boy of the Grenadier Guards, at this time he was seven years old. Destined for a military career, he became a field marshal in 1902, and later was Governor General of Canada. In 1879 he married Princess Louise Margaret, daughter of Prince Friedrich Karl of Prussia.

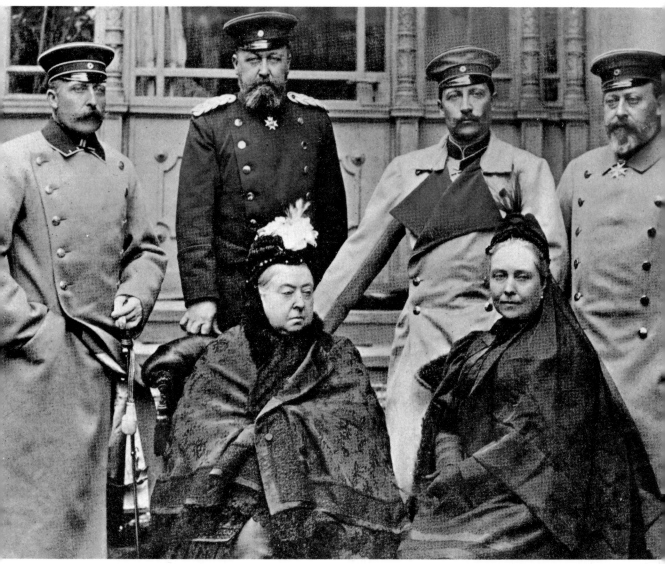

30 *Left* **Field Marshal HRH Prince George, Duke of Cambridge and Earl of Tipperary**
Eldest son of Adolphus, Duke of Cambridge and grandson of King George III, he was Commander-in-Chief of the British Army from 1856 to 1895. He is wearing the uniform as Colonel-in-Chief of the Rifle Brigade. Queen Victoria, his cousin, habitually referred to him as 'poor George', owing to his gift for making bad situations worse. He was a suitor for the Queen's hand in his younger days, but Queen Victoria then described him as 'that odious boy with an ugly face'. He was created Field Marshal in 1862, and eventually married Louisa Fairbrother, a well-known actress of the time, in contravention of the Royal Marriages Act.

31 Queen Victoria at Coburg with her family, 1894
Queen Victoria is pictured with her eldest daughter, the widowed Empress Victoria of Germany. From left to right are the Queen's sons: Prince Arthur, Duke of Connaught and Strathearn, Colonel of the Zieten Hussar Regiment No. 3; Prince Alfred, Duke of Edinburgh, Colonel of the Ninth Rheinisches Hussar Regiment; the Queen's eldest grandson, the Emperor Wilhelm II of Germany, King of Prussia and Colonel of the Life Guard Hussars and the Queen's eldest son, Edward Prince of Wales, Colonel of the Furst Blucher von Wahlstatt (Pomeranian) Hussar Regiment No. 5.

32 *Left* **Queen Victoria at luncheon, Windsor Castle, 1895**

Queen Victoria is sitting between her youngest daughter Princess Beatrice and Prince Heinrich of Battenberg, her husband. From left to right are their sons Prince Leopold and Prince Alexander, who renounced the title of Battenberg and was created Marquis of Carisbrooke by King George V in 1917. The little girl is their daughter Princess Victoria Eugénie, who married Alphonso XIII of Spain in 1906. Behind the Queen are her two Indian servants. The children are suitably enveloped in large table napkins and each has his or her own silver mug.

33   The Tsar and Tsarina's visit to Balmoral, 1896

The Tsar and Tsarina of All The Russias paid a private visit to Queen Victoria at Balmoral Castle in 1896. Tsar Nikolai II stands behind the Queen's carriage, with Tsarina Alexandra at the rear. Behind the carriage is Princess Helena Victoria of Schleswig-Holstein, the Queen's third daughter. John Brown, the Queen's servant, holds the pony's head. In front stands the Queen's son, Prince Arthur, Duke of Connaught and Strathearn. The Duchess is behind the Tsarina. The two young daughters of the Duke and Duchess are Princess Margaret, the eldest, who married King Gustaf Adolf VI of Sweden, and Princess Patricia, who married Admiral Sir Alexander Ramsay, son of the Thirteenth Earl of Dalhousie. The fat dog sitting on the carriage running-board is Turry, one of the Queen's favourites.

34 *Left* **Queen Victoria's Diamond Jubilee, 22 June 1897**
On 23 September 1896, Queen Victoria surpassed the achievement of George III, whose reign of fifty-nine years had been the longest in British history. Moreover, she had worn her crown almost twice as long as any reigning monarch, with the exception of Emperor Franz Josef of Austria. The occasion was marked by an imperial pageant of unsurpassed splendour, displaying the might and sheer geographical size of the Empire.

35 **Queen Victoria with her great grandsons, at Osborne, Isle of Wight, 1900**
Standing by the Queen's side is Prince Albert George, later Edward VIII, and subsequently Duke of Windsor. The baby in her arms is Prince Henry, Duke of Gloucester. Both were sons of Prince George, Duke of Cornwall and York, who succeeded his father Edward VII in 1910 as George V.

36 Queen Victoria's Diamond Jubilee, 22 June 1897

The royal carriage is just leaving Buckingham Palace, with a Guard of Honour drawn up on the forecourt. On the far side are soldiers of the Foot Guards, and on the near side sailors of the Royal Navy in summer rig, which at this time included the sennet hat. Just behind the carriage rides the Commander-in-Chief of the British Army, HRH George, Duke of Cambridge.

37 Officers on HMS Crescent awaiting Queen Victoria, 1898
Prince George, Duke of Cornwall and York stands second from the right. The Prince hoisted his pennant as Captain of the first-class cruiser *HMS Crescent* in June 1898. In 1889 he had commanded torpedo boat No. 79, and in the next year the gunboat Thrush. In 1891 he was promoted to commander, and served on HMS Melampus. He was promoted to captain in 1893.

38 Edward, Prince of Wales with a shooting party in Scotland, 1870
The guests are gathered around a shooting brake, at the entrance to Abergeldie Castle, a place frequently rented by the Prince during the season. He can be seen standing third from the right wearing a kilt. The stout gentleman leaning on his stick third from the left is Prince Edward of Saxe-Weimar-Eisenach, a younger son of the reigning Grand Duke. He joined the British Army as a career and became eventually Colonel of the First Life Guards, and a General. He married a daughter of the Fifth Duke of Richmond.

39 *Right* Children of the Prince and Princess of Wales, 1871
At the back stands their eldest son Prince Albert Victor, Duke of Clarence and Avondale, who died of pneumonia in 1892. Next to him is his youngest sister Princess Maud who became the first Queen of an independent Norway. In the middle is the eldest daughter Princess Louise, who married Alexander Duff, first Duke of Fife. Seated on the bottom left is Princess Victoria who remained unmarried, and on the right is Prince George, who was to become George V.

**40   HRH the Princess of Wales and favourite
dogs on board the Royal Yacht at Osborne, 1880**
Princess Alexandra of Wales was the eldest daughter
of King Christian IX of Denmark, and had married
Edward Prince of Wales in 1863. Her younger sister
marrried Tsar Alexander III of All The Russias. A
beautiful and elegant lady, Princess Alexandra had
five children. The eldest and heir to the throne,
Albert Edward, Duke of Clarence died in 1892 at the
age of twenty-eight and so his younger brother
succeeded as George V in 1910.

**41 Edward, Prince of Wales on Church Parade
at Windsor, 1898**
The Prince had been appointed Colonel-in-Chief of
the three regiments of household cavalry in 1880.
These regiments regularly rotated their quarters,
with two always in London, and the third at Windsor.
The Prince can be seen in the centre of the
photograph, surrounded by his officers. Headed by
the band, the regiment is marching from the Windsor
Parish Church to Combermere Barracks.

42 *Left* **Edward, Prince of Wales, 1890**
The Prince is wearing the uniform of Colonel-in-Chief of the Fifth Furst Blucher Von Wahlstatt (Pommeranian) Prussian Hussar Regiment. It was the custom for royalty to become Colonels-in-Chief of foreign regiments as a token of friendship and esteem. For instance, the Prussian Crown Prince was Colonel-in-Chief of the British 11th Prince Albert's own Hussars. Grand Duke Mikhael of Russia presented his Prussian Hussar Regiment with silver kettle drums to mark the occasion of his fiftieth year as Colonel-in-Chief. This honour was not restricted to men only; the Grand Duchess of Mecklenburg-Schwerin was Colonel-in-Chief of the Imperial German 18th Dragoon Regiment. In Russia, the Tsar's daughters became Colonels-in-Chief at birth, and in Spain, Queen Victoria Eugenie was Colonel-in-Chief of several regiments.

43 *Right,* **Edward, Prince of Wales, 1897**
Shown at the Duke and Duchess of Devonshire's historic ball given in celebration of Queen Victoria's Diamond Jubilee in 1897, the Prince is dressed as a Grand Master of the Knight Hospitallers of Malta. The costume was made by the theatrical costumiers L. and H. Nathan, and is still in their possession. They are now known as Bermans and Nathans Ltd of London.

44 *Left* **Edward VII and Queen Alexandra at Cowes for the Annual Regatta, 1903**
The King carried off many prizes with his famous yacht Britannia. He won the Queen's Cup five times, keeping the trophies for himself, but distributing the prize money amongst the crew. His mother Queen Victoria had built a house here, Osborne, and in fact died there in 1901. King Edward, however, was not at all attached to the property and did not use it much during his lifetime.

45 *Right* **Edward VII at the Derby of 1909**
The King looks well pleased with himself, having just won the Derby with his horse Minoru. He had a previous Derby winner in 1896 with Persimmon, who also won the St Leger in the same year. The King had registered his colours in 1875 as purple, gold band, scarlet sleeves and a black cap. The King won all the classic races of the turf, except the Oaks.

46 **Edward VII and Queen Alexandra on a visit to Dublin, 1907**
This visit was for an exhibition in what is now Herbert Park. Also in the carriage are the Viceroy and Vicereign, the Marquis and Marchioness of Aberdeen. He had previously served a term as Viceroy of Ireland in 1886.

ITALY

In the mid nineteenth century Italy was composed of the Duchies of Modena, Parma and Tuscany, together with the Kingdoms of Sardinia and the two Sicilies.

All these states were eventually to be drawn into one united Kingdom of Italy under the King of Sardinia, Vittorio Emanuele II, in 1861. This began with the defeat of the Austrians, who lost all their Italian possessions except Venice to the Sardinians, who then swallowed up the Duchies of Modena, Parma and Tuscany. The Nationalists all over Italy then rallied to Vittorio Emanuele, who sent Garibaldi to Sicily to help the revolutionaries there against their Bourbon King. Venice also fell to the Italians in 1866 after the Austro-Prussian war. Rome, the final independent state, offered only a token resistance to the Italian Army, and the King took up residence in the Quirinal Palace. He reigned until 1878.

His son Umberto I was not of the same calibre as his father, but managed to hold the kingdom together until he was assassinated in 1900. Vittorio Emanuele III, Umberto's only son, was an astute and educated man, although small in stature. During the First World War he endeared himself to the army by his constant visits to the trenches, where he was often under fire. His eldest son Umberto II, the last King of Italy, succeeded to the throne in 1946.

The Kingdom of the two Sicilies was ruled in the mid-nineteenth century by King Ferdinando II, a much maligned man who introduced many scientific advances to his kingdom. Unfortunately he was ugly, fat and coarse of feature, which did not help his public image. However, he did remain on his throne until 1859, when he was succeeded by his weak and melancholy son Francesco II.

Francesco II was no match for Garibaldi and the revolutionaries when they landed in Sicily. His hesitation meant that an invasion of the mainland quickly followed. Deserted by most of their followers, the royal family and their remaining loyal troops retired to the fortress of Gaeta, where they endured a three-month siege. In February 1861, they could hold out no longer, and so surrendered. The royal family then retired to the safety of Rome, and thence to Paris, where the King died in 1894.

ITALY

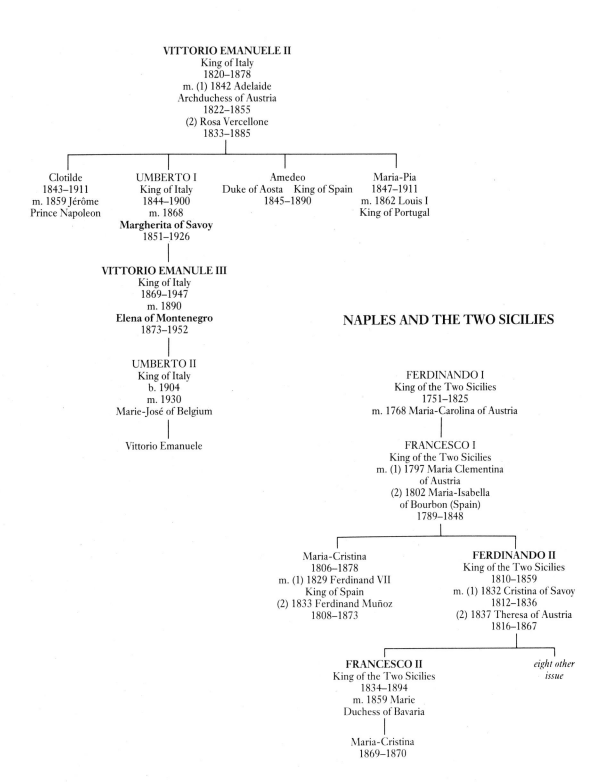

VITTORIO EMANUELE II
King of Italy
1820–1878
m. (1) 1842 Adelaide
Archduchess of Austria
1822–1855
(2) Rosa Vercellone
1833–1885

Clotilde
1843–1911
m. 1859 Jérôme
Prince Napoleon

UMBERTO I
King of Italy
1844–1900
m. 1868
Margherita of Savoy
1851–1926

Amedeo
Duke of Aosta   King of Spain
1845–1890

Maria-Pia
1847–1911
m. 1862 Louis I
King of Portugal

VITTORIO EMANULE III
King of Italy
1869–1947
m. 1890
Elena of Montenegro
1873–1952

UMBERTO II
King of Italy
b. 1904
m. 1930
Marie-José of Belgium

Vittorio Emanuele

NAPLES AND THE TWO SICILIES

FERDINANDO I
King of the Two Sicilies
1751–1825
m. 1768 Maria-Carolina of Austria

FRANCESCO I
King of the Two Sicilies
m. (1) 1797 Maria Clementina
of Austria
(2) 1802 Maria-Isabella
of Bourbon (Spain)
1789–1848

Maria-Cristina
1806–1878
m. (1) 1829 Ferdinand VII
King of Spain
(2) 1833 Ferdinand Muñoz
1808–1873

FERDINANDO II
King of the Two Sicilies
1810–1859
m. (1) 1832 Cristina of Savoy
1812–1836
(2) 1837 Theresa of Austria
1816–1867

FRANCESCO II
King of the Two Sicilies
1834–1894
m. 1859 Marie
Duchess of Bavaria

*eight other
issue*

Maria-Cristina
1869–1870

47 *Left* **Vittorio Emanuele II, King of Italy,**
c. **1861**
Known as 'the gentleman king'; when not engaged in field sports, he chased women. When he became a widower, he married his mistress, a lusty drum-major's daughter, 'La Rosina', whom he created Countess Mirafiori e Fontana-Fredda. He was a natural actor, who progressed from King of Sardinia to King of a united Italy, after the nationalistic revolutions had swept the House of Savoy onto the throne. The king unfortunately died of pneumonia in 1878, at the early age of fifty-seven.

48   Queen Margherita of Italy, 1875
The wife of King Umberto I, Queen Margherita was said to have the face of an angel. She was also artistic, tall and fair-haired, and dominated her husband. The second wife and also the cousin of King Umberto, Margherita was the only daughter of Prince Fernando of Savoy, Duke of Genoa. The King was assassinated at Monza by an anarchist in 1900 and was succeeded by their only child Vittorio Emmanuele III.

49 *Left* **Vittorio Emanuele III and Queen Elena of Italy, November 1903**
Vittorio Emanuele succeeded his father in 1900 and reigned until 1946. He was an astute and well educated man, but so short in stature his feet did not touch the floor when he sat on the throne. He did however marry for love – the tall Princess Elena of Montenegro. In the First World War, the King spent all the time with his troops at the front and appointed his cousin to act as regent.

50 Ferdinando II, King of the Two Sicilies, 1859
Ferdinando succeeded to the throne in 1830 and died in 1859 at the age of forty-nine. Much maligned by the European press and politicians, particularly Gladstone, he did, however, introduce railways and electricity and the kingdom prospered. The King was inclined to stoutness, and his coarse features did nothing for his public image, as can be seen from this photograph.

51 *Left* **Francesco II, King of the Two Sicilies, 1859**

Francesco succeeded his father Ferdinando II in 1859, and lost his kingdom when it was annexed to the new Kingdom of Italy in 1860. Pale, melancholy, and indecisive in politics, he lost his throne in two years. The King is wearing the uniform of captain-general of the Neapolitan Army.

52 **Francesco II, King of the Two Sicilies, kneels to receive the blessing of Pope Pius IX, Rome, 1861**

Having lost his kingdom to Garibaldi and the army of unity, Francesco retired to Rome, where the royal family lived until 1870, when they moved to Paris.

BELGIUM

THE NETHERLANDS AND LUXEMBOURG

When Belgium broke away from the Netherlands in 1830, they invited Prince Leopold of Saxe-Coburg-Saalfeld to be their king. The Prince had been married to George IV's daughter Charlotte. Her death in childbirth had put paid to his thoughts of being Prince Consort of Great Britain. Uncle to Queen Victoria, he held a special place in her esteem, although he did not influence her decisions as much as he thought he did. When Queen Louise died in 1851, he found consolation in the arms of his former mistress, Madam Meyer Von Eppinghoven. This liaison lasted until his death in 1865.

His son Leopold II had cold eyes, a large nose and a way of making money which made him one of the richest monarchs in Europe. He also had a scandalous private life with many liaisons, that made him unpopular with his subjects. His only son had died at the age of ten. His eldest daughter Stephanie had married the Crown Prince Rudolf of Austria who shot himself. Louise, the second daughter was no happier, having married Prince Philip of Saxe-Coburg and Gotha, whose reputation was not of the best and who had curious sexual tastes. The Princess found consolation in the arms of Count Mattachich, a Hungarian. Her husband had her locked up in an asylum, from which the Count romantically rescued her. The youngest daughter Clementine married Prince Victor Napoleon, against the wishes of her father who did not want to offend the neighbouring French Republic, nor jeopardise his customary visits to Paris and the Riviera. The King died in 1909, and was succeeded by his nephew Albert I, a tall soldierly figure, who quickly became popular with his people. When Belgium was invaded in 1914 the King put himself at the head of his army and was in the thick of the fighting earning himself the title of 'Roi Chevalier'. Tragically, he died in a mountaineering accident in 1934.

Willem III, King of the Netherlands came to the throne in 1849. He had three sons by his marriage to Princess Sophie of Wurttemberg, but they all died before their father. The two elder Princes had not married, preferring the gay life of Paris during the Second Empire, where their names were linked to many of the courtesans of the time. King Willem was then forced to find a wife, if the House of Orange was to continue to rule Holland. He eventually chose Emma, daughter of the Prince of Waldeck and Pyrmont, and a daughter was born in the following year. The King died in 1890, when his daughter Wilhelmina was only ten years old. She ruled under the regency of her mother Queen Emma until she came of age in 1898. Queen Wilhelmina ruled for the next fifty years. In 1901 she married Prince Heinrich of Mecklenburg Schwerin, and their daughter Princess Juliana was born in 1909.

Although the laws of the Netherlands permitted the succession to the throne to pass through the female line, the laws of the Grand Duchy of Luxembourg did not, and so when King Willem died, his Duchy passed to the elder branch of the House of Nassau. The Duchy of Nassau had sided with Austria in the Austro-Prussian war of 1866, and on their defeat the Duchy was annexed by victorious Prussia. The reigning Duke, Adolphe, lived in exile. It was not until the death of King Willem's third son that it was certain that he would inherit the Grand Duchy of Luxembourg; a pleasant compensation for the loss of Nassau. He was over seventy when he came to the throne, but lived on until the age of eighty-eight, having enjoyed fifteen years as the ruler of the Grand Duchy. The Grand Duke had married Elizabeth of Russia in 1844, but she died without children a year later. In 1851 Grand Duke Adolphe married Princess Adelheid of Anhalt, and a son and heir was born the following year. Grand Duke Guillaume IV succeeded his father in 1905, and reigned for seven years. He married Maria Anna, Infanta of Portugal, who bore him six children, all girls.

When the Grand Duke died in 1912, a family statute permitted the eldest daughter to inherit the Grand Duchy, which had previously been bound by Salic law, and Adelheid became Grand Duchess at the age of eighteen. Two years later the German army marched into the Grand Duchy. Having fallen foul of both sides in the First World War, the Grand Duchess abdicated in 1919, in favour of her sister Charlotte, who reigned for the next forty-five years.

THE NETHERLANDS

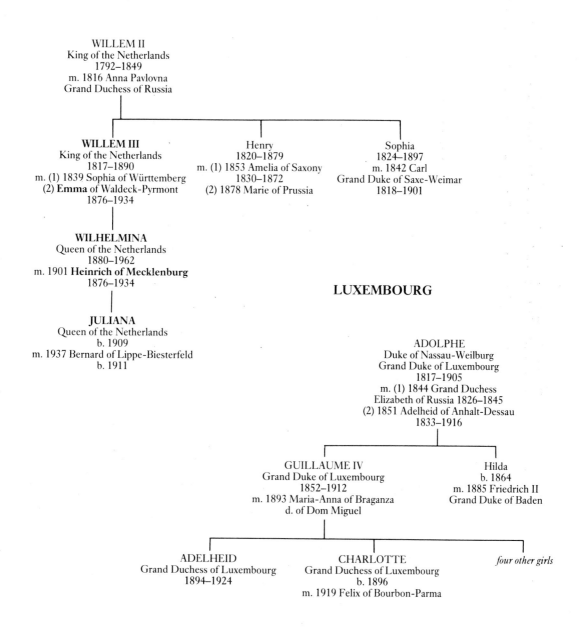

WILLEM II
King of the Netherlands
1792–1849
m. 1816 Anna Pavlovna
Grand Duchess of Russia

WILLEM III
King of the Netherlands
1817–1890
m. (1) 1839 Sophia of Württemberg
(2) **Emma** of Waldeck-Pyrmont
1876–1934

Henry
1820–1879
m. (1) 1853 Amelia of Saxony
1830–1872
(2) 1878 Marie of Prussia

Sophia
1824–1897
m. 1842 Carl
Grand Duke of Saxe-Weimar
1818–1901

WILHELMINA
Queen of the Netherlands
1880–1962
m. 1901 **Heinrich of Mecklenburg**
1876–1934

JULIANA
Queen of the Netherlands
b. 1909
m. 1937 Bernard of Lippe-Biesterfeld
b. 1911

LUXEMBOURG

ADOLPHE
Duke of Nassau-Weilburg
Grand Duke of Luxembourg
1817–1905
m. (1) 1844 Grand Duchess
Elizabeth of Russia 1826–1845
(2) 1851 Adelheid of Anhalt-Dessau
1833–1916

GUILLAUME IV
Grand Duke of Luxembourg
1852–1912
m. 1893 Maria-Anna of Braganza
d. of Dom Miguel

Hilda
b. 1864
m. 1885 Friedrich II
Grand Duke of Baden

ADELHEID
Grand Duchess of Luxembourg
1894–1924

CHARLOTTE
Grand Duchess of Luxembourg
b. 1896
m. 1919 Felix of Bourbon-Parma

four other girls

BELGIUM

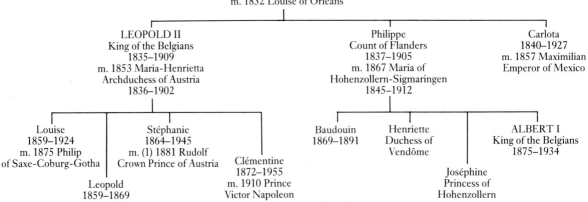

LEOPOLD I
King of the Belgians
1790–1865
m. 1832 Louise of Orléans

LEOPOLD II
King of the Belgians
1835–1909
m. 1853 Maria-Henrietta
Archduchess of Austria
1836–1902

Philippe
Count of Flanders
1837–1905
m. 1867 Maria of
Hohenzollern-Sigmaringen
1845–1912

Carlota
1840–1927
m. 1857 Maximilian
Emperor of Mexico

Louise
1859–1924
m. 1875 Philip
of Saxe-Coburg-Gotha

Stéphanie
1864–1945
m. (1) 1881 Rudolf
Crown Prince of Austria

Leopold
1859–1869

Clémentine
1872–1955
m. 1910 Prince
Victor Napoleon

Baudouin
1869–1891

Henriette
Duchess of
Vendôme

Joséphine
Princess of
Hohenzollern

ALBERT I
King of the Belgians
1875–1934

53 *Left* **Leopold I, King of the Belgians, 1857**
Prince Leopold was the third son of the Duke of
Saxe-Coburg-Saafeld. He had married George IV's
daughter Charlotte and but for her untimely death in
childbirth, he would have been Prince Consort of
Great Britain. When the Belgians broke away from
Holland in 1830, they invited him to be their king. His
sister was Queen Victoria's mother.

54 **Willem, Prince of Orange, *c.* 1870**
Eldest son of King Willem II of the Netherlands, he
found the sophisticated life of Paris during the
Second Empire more entertaining than that of the
Hague. In contemporary memoirs, the Prince's name
is continually linked with the famous of the time,
particuarly Cora Pearl, whom he supported for some
time before her liaison with the Duc de Morny. He
was irreverently called 'Prince Citron', because of his
yellowish complexion. His excesses led in fact to his
premature death in 1879, at the age of thirty-nine. He
was unmarried, and this, coupled with the deaths of
his two brothers, meant that his father was obliged to
marry again to produce an heir to the House of
Orange.

55 *Opposite* **Willem III, King of the Netherlands and Grand Duke of Luxembourg, 1880**
The King married Princess Sophie of Württemburg in 1839 and they had three sons, all of whom predeceased him, as did his three younger brothers, none of them leaving any children. When the Queen died in 1877, the King sought the hand of a Princess amongst the Courts of Europe and eventually found Princess Emma of Waldeck and Pyrmont. The King is wearing the uniform of a Colonel of Hussars.

56 *Left* **Queen Emma of the Netherlands, 1880**
The young girl with a twinkle in her eye is Princess Emma of Waldeck and Pyrmont who married Willem III of the Netherlands when she was only nineteen and he was sixty-two. A daughter, Princess Wilhelmina, was born the following year. Queen Emma was Regent of the Netherlands after King Willem's death in 1890, until her daughter came of age.

57   Queen Wilhelmina of the Netherlands on manoeuvres with her army, *c.* 1900

The Queen is riding side-saddle, and behind her can be seen staff officers, the feathers of their cocked hats flying in the wind. At this time the Dutch Army consisted of 64,000 men. The Colonial Army, consisting entirely of volunteers, numbered about 30,000 men. The Netherlands had declared itself a neutral state, and her energy was devoted to furthering her commercial and colonial interests. The Army was confined to the business of national defence.

58   Queen Wilhelmina of the Netherlands on board a Dutch warship, *c.* **1913**
The Queen and her daughter, Princess Juliana, are surrounded by her naval and marine officers. Seated next to her, in admiral's uniform, is her husband, Prince Heinrich of Mecklenburg-Schwerin, who was the youngest of eight brothers. His father, Grand Duke Friedrich Franz II, was married three times.

PRUSSIA

AND THE GERMAN EMPIRE

In 1848 Prussia received her first Parliament under King Friedrich Wilhelm IV. The state had been modernised and the army rebuilt after the Napoleonic Wars. The European revolutions of 1848 had forced the King to create an elected parliament, although he was able to crush the revolutionaries with his model army. Germany was already moving towards a confederation and the Imperial crown was offered to Friedrich Wilhelm, but he refused. After a stroke that left him incapacitated, his brother Wilhelm succeeded to the Prussian throne.

It was he who appointed Prince Bismarck as Chancellor, and under his leadership Prussia was set on the road to imperial power. Firstly Denmark was crushed in 1864, in the war over the Duchy of Schleswig-Holstein. Secondly, Austria was defeated in the war of 1866 and lost her hold over Germany, and finally France. The glittering Empire was soundly beaten within a few weeks in 1870. King Wilhelm was proclaimed Wilhelm I, Emperor of Germany, at Versailles, the palace of the fallen French Emperor.

When Wilhelm died in 1888, he was succeeded by his sickly son Friedrich, son-in-law of Queen Victoria. He died within the year and was succeeded by his dynamic son Wilhelm II, who was to dominate Europe until the catastrophe of 1914. One of his first acts was to dismiss Bismarck. He was a busy man, always in the public eye, forever in uniform as he travelled about the Empire, basking in the publicity that he attracted. He was a great "sabre rattler" which made him unpopular with the British people, whom he actually admired greatly. His rivalry with the British drove them into an *entente* with the French, with whom they had less affinity.

The mid-nineteenth century in Bavaria was dominated by the insane King Ludwig II who had succeeded to the throne at the age of nineteen. His friendship with Wagner made Munich a cultural centre, and he put vast sums of money at the composer's disposal enabling him to complete "The Ring" and "Parsifal". King Ludwig built several magnificent palaces and castles, particularly Neuschwanstein, a fairy castle perched on a mountain top, and Herrenchiemse, his replica of Versailles. The Government viewed all this squandering of the exchequer with alarm. His friendships with Wagner and later with a young actor and his groom were also cause for unease. He was engaged for a short while to his cousin Princess Sophie but this was broken off. He became a recluse, increasingly despondent and gloomy. Eventually he was declared insane and removed to the Castle of Berg, where he drowned in the lake under mysterious circumstances, together with the doctor who had declared him insane.

Ludwig II was succeeded by his brother Otto, who had been mentally unbalanced since 1871. The country was therefore placed under the regency of their unpopular uncle, Prince Luitpold. He died in 1912 and was succeeded in the following year by his son Ludwig III. King Otto was legally deposed in 1913 and died in 1916.

The kings of Hanover were descended from Queen Victoria's uncle, Ernest Augustus, Duke of Cumberland who had succeeded to the throne because of the Salic law. The Kingdom of Hanover was conquered by the Prussians in 1866 and annexed as King George V had come to the aid of Austria when Prussia declared war against those who had signed the Diet of Confederations in favour of Austria. The Royal Family lived in exile on their Austrian estates, in bitter hatred of the Prussians. The family feud was not brought to a conciliatory conclusion until the marriage in 1913 of the Emperor Wilhelm II's daughter and the Hanoverian heir.

The Kingdom of Saxony had lost two-thirds of its territory as a result of accepting and supporting Napoleon I, Emperor of the French. King Antony Clement himself had been captured and the whole country might have been given to Prussia, but for the intervention of Austria. The rest of the nineteenth century passed quietly. The revolutions of 1849 brought a constitution; once again Saxony fought on the losing side in the War of 1866, but fortunately this did not result in the loss of any more territories. In the Franco-Prussian War of 1870, Saxony was on the side of Prussia, and King Albert distinguished himself as a General in the Allied army.

Württemburg also fought for Napoleon, but King Frederick I joined the Allied side after the Battle of Leipzig in 1813 and was thus able to preserve the kingdom. In the 1866 war, Württemburg sided with Austria, but defeat required only the payment of an indemnity to Prussia. Thus the century passed comparatively quietly at the Court in Stuttgart.

The thirty or so other German states were ruled by Grand Dukes, Princes and Dukes. Some were quite large, such as the Grand Duchy of Baden, or the Duchy of Mecklenburg-Schwerin; others were very small, consisting of a few square miles, such as the Saxon Duchies. But each was individual with its own court and army, albeit one or two regiments.

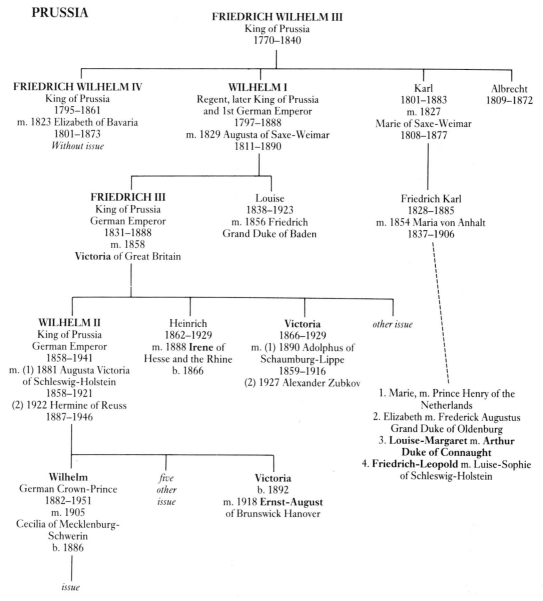

PRUSSIA

FRIEDRICH WILHELM III
King of Prussia
1770–1840

FRIEDRICH WILHELM IV
King of Prussia
1795–1861
m. 1823 Elizabeth of Bavaria
1801–1873
Without issue

WILHELM I
Regent, later King of Prussia
and 1st German Emperor
1797–1888
m. 1829 Augusta of Saxe-Weimar
1811–1890

Karl
1801–1883
m. 1827
Marie of Saxe-Weimar
1808–1877

Albrecht
1809–1872

FRIEDRICH III
King of Prussia
German Emperor
1831–1888
m. 1858
Victoria of Great Britain

Louise
1838–1923
m. 1856 Friedrich
Grand Duke of Baden

Friedrich Karl
1828–1885
m. 1854 Maria von Anhalt
1837–1906

WILHELM II
King of Prussia
German Emperor
1858–1941
m. (1) 1881 Augusta Victoria
of Schleswig-Holstein
1858–1921
(2) 1922 Hermine of Reuss
1887–1946

Heinrich
1862–1929
m. 1888 **Irene** of
Hesse and the Rhine
b. 1866

Victoria
1866–1929
m. (1) 1890 Adolphus of
Schaumburg-Lippe
1859–1916
(2) 1927 Alexander Zubkov

other issue

1. Marie, m. Prince Henry of the
Netherlands
2. Elizabeth m. Frederick Augustus
Grand Duke of Oldenburg
3. **Louise-Margaret** m. **Arthur
Duke of Connaught**
4. **Friedrich-Leopold** m. Luise-Sophie
of Schleswig-Holstein

Wilhelm
German Crown-Prince
1882–1951
m. 1905
Cecilia of Mecklenburg-
Schwerin
b. 1886

*five
other
issue*

Victoria
b. 1892
m. 1918 **Ernst-August**
of Brunswick Hanover

issue

HANOVER

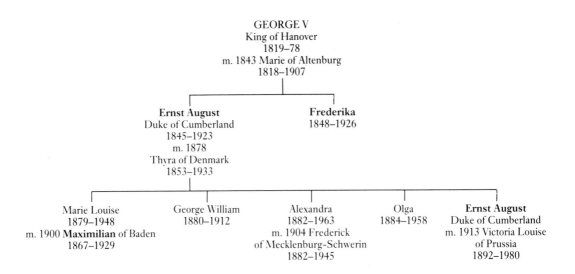

GEORGE V
King of Hanover
1819–78
m. 1843 Marie of Altenburg
1818–1907

Ernst August
Duke of Cumberland
1845–1923
m. 1878
Thyra of Denmark
1853–1933

Frederika
1848–1926

Marie Louise
1879–1948
m. 1900 **Maximilian** of Baden
1867–1929

George William
1880–1912

Alexandra
1882–1963
m. 1904 Frederick
of Mecklenburg-Schwerin
1882–1945

Olga
1884–1958

Ernst August
Duke of Cumberland
m. 1913 Victoria Louise
of Prussia
1892–1980

BADEN

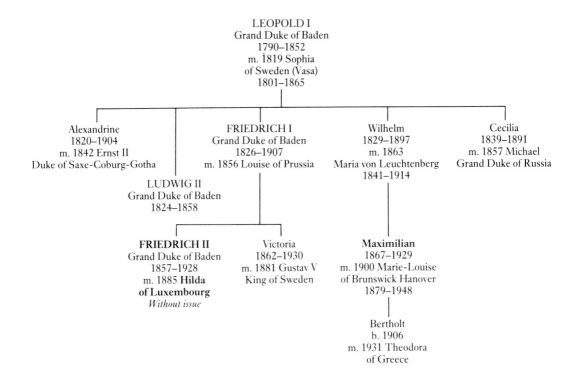

LEOPOLD I
Grand Duke of Baden
1790–1852
m. 1819 Sophia
of Sweden (Vasa)
1801–1865

Alexandrine
1820–1904
m. 1842 Ernst II
Duke of Saxe-Coburg-Gotha

FRIEDRICH I
Grand Duke of Baden
1826–1907
m. 1856 Louise of Prussia

Wilhelm
1829–1897
m. 1863
Maria von Leuchtenberg
1841–1914

Cecilia
1839–1891
m. 1857 Michael
Grand Duke of Russia

LUDWIG II
Grand Duke of Baden
1824–1858

FRIEDRICH II
Grand Duke of Baden
1857–1928
m. 1885 **Hilda**
of Luxembourg
Without issue

Victoria
1862–1930
m. 1881 Gustav V
King of Sweden

Maximilian
1867–1929
m. 1900 Marie-Louise
of Brunswick Hanover
1879–1948

Bertholt
b. 1906
m. 1931 Theodora
of Greece

59 King Friedrich Wilhelm IV, King of Prussia, c. 1850

He became King in 1840, and extended Prussian influence over the rest of Germany, but refused to become Emperor of Germany. In 1857 the King became incapacitated following a stroke, and his brother and future successor Wilhelm I took over. At this period the famous German helmet 'the picklehaube' was introduced and one can be seen in the King's hand.

60 Prince Wilhelm of Prussia, 1874

The future Kaiser Wilhelm II of Germany, King of Prussia, photographed at the age of fifteen, when he was enrolled in the First Regiment of Footguards. He succeeded to the Imperial throne at the age of twenty-eight, after the ninety-eight day reign of his father, the Emperor Friedrich III, in 1888. Thus the year that had started with Emperor Wilhelm I's death at the age of ninety-one, ended with the accession of the youthful and promising Wilhelm II.

61 Prince Friedrich Leopold of Prussia (left) on his bicycle, *c.* 1880
Prince Friedrich was the eldest son of Prince Friedrich Karl of Prussia. He was born in 1865 and married Princess Luise Sophie of Schleswig-Holstein-Sonderburg-Augustenburg, whose sister, Auguste Victoria, married Wilhelm II, Emperor of Germany, King of Prussia.

62 *Right* Four Generations of the Hohenzollerns, 1882
Emperor Wilhelm I of Germany, King of Prussia, is seated holding his great-grandson Prince Wilhelm. On the left stands Crown Prince Friedrich, who succeeded his father as Emperor in 1888, and reigned for only ninety-eight days before dying of throat cancer. On the right stands his eldest son Prince Wilhelm (the future Kaiser Wilhelm II), his malformed arm thrust into the pocket of his hussar jacket.

63 Royal Group after watching army manoeuvres, 20 September, 1883

A group of royal guests at Castle Homburg. The ladies (left to right) are: Princess Victoria of Hesse and by Rhine, Louise, Duchess of Connaught and Strathearn, Princess Elizabeth of Hesse and by Rhine, her sister Princess Irene (just obscured), Princess Victoria of Prussia, and Victoria, Crown Princess of Prussia. From the left, the gentlemen are: the hereditary Grand Duke of Saxe-Weimar-Eisenach; King Milan of Serbia; and Prince Arthur Duke of Connaught and Strathearn. In front is the Emperor Wilhelm I of Germany, King of Prussia, with Crown Prince Carlos of Portugal behind him and King Alfonso XII of Spain on the Emperor's left. Prince Wilhelm of Prussia is behind King Leopold. George Duke of Cambridge has the white side-whiskers; next to him are Grand Duke Ludwig IV of Hesse and by Rhine, Grand Duke Hermann of Saxe-Weimar-Eisenach, Crown Prince Friedrich of Prussia, King Albert of Saxony (in the light-coloured uniform) and Albert Edward, Prince of Wales.

64 *Above, left* **Emperor Friedrich III of Germany, 1888**

Queen Victoria's son-in-law, having married her eldest daughter Victoria, the Princess Royal, in 1858. When he succeeded his father, the Emperor Wilhelm I, Friedrich was already mortally ill with throat cancer and died after a reign of ninety-eight days. He was succeeded by his eldest son, Wilhelm II, who was twenty-eight years old. The Emperor wears the uniform of the 2nd Kurrassier Regiment, and carries in his right hand the baton of a Field Marshal of Prussia.

65 *Above, right* **Princess Louise Margaret, Duchess of Connaught and Strathearn, 14 September 1890**

The Princess was the daughter of Prince Friedrich Karl of Prussia, and had married the third son of Queen Victoria, Arthur Duke of Connaught and Strathearn in 1879. It was the custom in the Imperial German Army for Royal Colonels-in-Chief to be appointed; this included ladies of royal blood. The Duchess is wearing the uniform of her own regiment, the 64th Prince Friedrich Karl of Prussia Regiment, named in honour of her father.

66 *Opposite* **Wilhelm II Emperor of Germany, King of Prussia, 1897**

Courtly and kind-hearted, a model husband and father, he liked to dominate and to show off the splendour of his brilliant court. His army was the finest in Europe and he liked nothing better than to review it. He was hardly ever photographed in civilian clothes, as he virtually lived in uniform. His left arm, withered at birth, made him determined to excel in all manly pursuits, and he consequently became a superb shot and excellent horseman. As the eldest grandson of Queen Victoria, he had a particular place in her affections. It was in Wilhelm's arms that she died at Osborne in 1901. The Kaiser is photographed in the uniform of Colonel-in-Chief of the Mounted Life Guards; the cuirass is of painted black iron, worn at the New Year parades.

67 *Left* **The Kaiser Wilhelm II of Germany, King of Prussia at a shooting party at Windsor November 1907**
The Kaiser and Kaiserin stand in the centre, greeting Louise, Duchess of Connaught and Strathearn, the daughter of Prince Friedrich Karl of Prussia. Behind her are her daughters, Princess Patricia, who later married Admiral Sir Alexander Ramsay, and Princess Margaret who was to marry Gustaf Adolf Crown Prince of Sweden; their brother, Prince Arthur of Connaught, is on the left talking to Queen Alexandra who has her back to the camera.

68 *Below* **The Emperor inspecting an infantry regiment, 1910**
The Emperor, Wilhelm II, King of Prussia is on the right, with his staff on the left, as he inspects the line of infantry drawn up in review. The German Army at this time was a large well-trained force, waiting for the call. The utter defeat of the French Army in the Franco-Prussian War of 1870 displayed how well the German Army had been prepared by Moltke and Bismarck.

69 *Left* **The Crown Prince Wilhelm of Prussia hunting with members of the Ducal Bavarian family near Kreuth, *c.* 1905**
Crown Prince Wilhelm of Prussia was the eldest son of the Emperor Wilhelm II of Germany, King of Prussia. He was a charming and popular young man, especially in England, where he spent time with his favourite uncle King Edward VII. He was an excellent rider and rode to hounds when he was staying with English friends. During the First World War, however, vindictive politicians launched a successful campaign to ruin his reputation.

70 *Left* **Alexander III Tsar and Autocrat of All The Russias at Berlin, 1889**
Fourth from the right stands the Emperor Wilhelm II of Germany, King of Prussia, in the uniform of a Russian General. Next to him stands the Tsar in German uniform. They are watching the march past of the German Honour Guard, during the state visit of the Tsar to Germany.

71   Ludwig I, King of Bavaria, 1860
Ludwig I was born in 1786 and was a godson of the ill-fated Queen of France, Marie Antoinette. Never able to resist a pretty face, he became involved with a Spanish dancer, Lola Montez in 1848. He created her Countess of Lansfeld, which caused great indignation amongst the Bavarian nobility. Eventually he was forced to abdicate in favour of his son Maximilian in 1848. One day when dining with the Empress Eugénie of France, whom he was complimenting on her beauty, he said 'Ah, the women of Spain. I know something about them. One of them even cost me my throne'. Ludwig died at Nice in the South of France in 1868.

72   The Prince of Waldeck and Pyrmont and his family in the drawing room of Castle Arolsen, 1877

Amongst the group is seated, third from left, Princess Emma who married King Willem III of the Netherlands. Next to the Princess, reading the paper, is her father, the ruling Prince Georg Viktor. The Prince Friedrich is standing behind his father. Princess Helena, who married in 1882 Prince Leopold, Duke of Albany, younger son of Queen Victoria, is standing centre.

73   *Right* King George V of Hanover, Duke of Cumberland and Teviotdale, 1865

Grandson of George III of Great Britain. He succeeded to the throne in 1851. He married Princess Marie of Saxe-Altenburg, and is seen here with two of their children: Princess Frederika, who married Baron Alfons von Pawel-Rammingen, and Crown Prince Ernst August. King George lost his sight in an accident when young. In the war of 1866 Hanover sided with Austria, but was soon beaten by the Prussians, and the royal family went into exile. King George spent most of the remaining years of his life in Austria, but died in Paris and was buried in St. George's Chapel, Windsor in 1878.

74 *Above, left* **Crown Prince Ernst August of Hanover, 1866**
Defeated and driven into exile by the Austro-Prussian War of 1866, the Prince lived the life of a gentleman on his Austrian estates. In 1878, he succeeded his father as head of the House of Hanover and in 1884 succeeded his kinsman as Duke of Brunswick. Due to the hostility of Bismarck he was unable to reign in Brunswick. He was forgotten by the world until the First World War, when he was struck off the roll of the Order of the Garter, and deprived of his peerages and titles in Great Britain. He died in 1923, at the age of 78.

75 *Above, right* **Ludwig IV, Grand Duke of Hesse and by Rhine with his wife, Princess Alice, second daughter of Queen Victoria, 1866**
The two little girls are their eldest daughters. On the left, Princess Elisabeth, who married Grand Duke Sergei of Russia. He was blown up by an anarchist

bomb in 1905 and the Princess was murdered by the Bolsheviks in 1918. On the right is Princess Victoria, who married Prince Louis of Battenberg, who was created First Marquis of Milford Haven by King George V of Great Britain, in 1917. His second son was Lord Louis Mountbatten of Burma.

76 *Right* **Friedrich Franz III Grand Duke of Mecklenburg-Schwerin, *c.* 1880**
The Grand Duke was married to the Grand Duchess Anastasia of Russia. His eldest daughter married the Crown Prince of Denmark, later King Christian X, and the younger one, Crown Prince Wilhelm II. A wealthy couple, the Grand Duke and Duchess spent five months of the year in the south of France, where the Grand Duchess's brother Grand Duke Michael of Russia was living in exile with his morganatic wife, Countess Torby. The Grand Duke Friedrich died at Cannes in 1897 and was succeeded by his only son.

77 Prince Maximilian of Baden, 1890
The Prince is wearing the uniform of the Prussian Lifeguards of which he was a serving officer. He was the cousin of the ruling Grand Duke Friedrich II and would have succeeded to the throne, but for the First World War. In 1900 he married Princess Marie Louise, eldest daughter of Ernst August, Crown Prince of Hanover, third Duke of Cumberland.

78 *Right* Wilhelm II, King of Württemburg, 1895
He succeeded his uncle Karl I, in 1891. A man of taste and a judge of good horseflesh, he kept the finest stud farm in Europe. The King was married twice, first to Princess Marie of Waldeck and Pyrmont, who died in 1882, after the birth of a stillborn daughter. Their other daughter, Princess Pauline, was born in 1877 and married Prince Wilhelm of Wied in 1898. The King's second wife was Princess Charlotte of Schaumberg Lippe whom he married in 1886. Unfortunately the couple were childless, which caused a dynastic crisis, as there were no direct male heirs to the throne (the Salic Law not permitting Princess Pauline to succeed). After the disaster of 1914 this problem was purely academic. The King is seen here in the uniform of Colonel-in-Chief of the Prussian Lifeguard Hussars.

79 Prince Friedrich Wilhelm of Baden, with his bride, Princess Hilda of Luxembourg, youngest daughter of Grand Duke Adolphe of Luxembourg, Duke of Nassau, 1885

Prince Friedrich succeeded as Grand Duke of Baden in 1907 on the death of his father. His sister, Victoria, married Crown Prince Gustaf of Sweden in 1881.

80 *Right* Prince Ernst August, Duke of Brunswick and Luneburg with his bride, Princess Victoria Luise of Germany and Prussia, 1913

Their wedding took place in Berlin and was the last great gathering of European royalty. It healed the breach between the German Emperor's family and the Brunswick Hanover family. (The Kingdom of Hanover having fallen to Prussia after the War of 1866, the King of Hanover succeeded to the Duchy of Brunswick in 1884, but was prevented by Bismarck from reigning there). As a wedding present Kaiser Wilhelm gave his son-in-law the Duchy of Brunswick, and so provided a happy ending to the story.

RUSSIA

The Romanoff family ruled Russia from 1613 until the Revolution of 1917. On the death of Nikolai I in 1855, just before the end of the Crimean War, his eldest son Alexander II ascended the throne. His reforms such as introducing trial by jury, emancipation of the serfs and expansion of the universities brought him the gratitude of many of his people. For some, the reforms were not enough, and the universities began to be the breeding ground of revolution. Just as he was about to set up a new Parliament, Alexander was assassinated in 1881.

The new Tsar, Alexander III, revoked all the reforms and introduced sterner measures to crush the revolutionaries. He was a large, powerfully built man, who did not think his people ready for political reform, but set out to modernise Russia and create a successful industrial nation. He was successful in this and for a time Russia was peaceful. He died prematurely in 1894 and was succeeded by his twenty-six year old son Nikolai II, a small, withdrawn and distant Tsar, not at all like his father. It was unfortunate that his wife, Tsarina Alexandra, was also cold, aloof and tight-lipped. Contemporaries say that the Tsarina was also haughty, always on the defensive and miserable. They were in fact both shy and had to be drawn out in conversation, and they were also both preoccupied with the poor health of the Tsarevitch Alexis, who had haemophilia, and was frequently ill and close to death. Society was thus without its natural leaders. The defeat of the Russian Army by the Japanese in 1904 was followed by the First World War, for which Russia was not prepared. Russia was overwhelmed by revolution which ended in the wholesale slaughter of the Imperial Family by the Communists.

RUSSIA

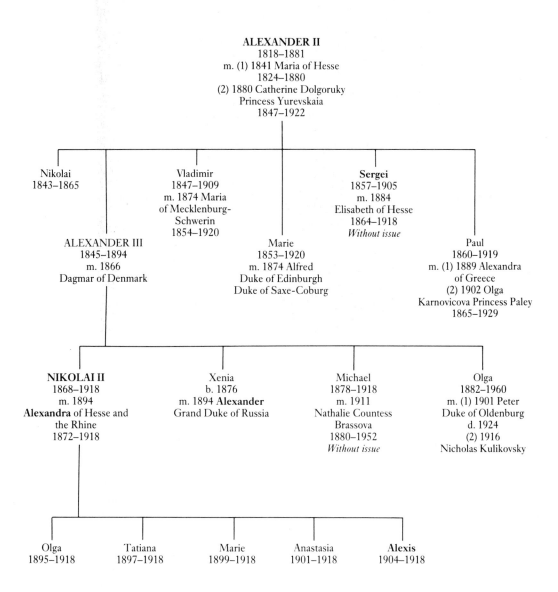

ALEXANDER II
1818–1881
m. (1) 1841 Maria of Hesse
1824–1880
(2) 1880 Catherine Dolgoruky
Princess Yurevskaia
1847–1922

Nikolai
1843–1865

Vladimir
1847–1909
m. 1874 Maria
of Mecklenburg-
Schwerin
1854–1920

Sergei
1857–1905
m. 1884
Elisabeth of Hesse
1864–1918
Without issue

ALEXANDER III
1845–1894
m. 1866
Dagmar of Denmark

Marie
1853–1920
m. 1874 Alfred
Duke of Edinburgh
Duke of Saxe-Coburg

Paul
1860–1919
m. (1) 1889 Alexandra
of Greece
(2) 1902 Olga
Karnovicova Princess Paley
1865–1929

NIKOLAI II
1868–1918
m. 1894
Alexandra of Hesse and
the Rhine
1872–1918

Xenia
b. 1876
m. 1894 **Alexander**
Grand Duke of Russia

Michael
1878–1918
m. 1911
Nathalie Countess
Brassova
1880–1952
Without issue

Olga
1882–1960
m. (1) 1901 Peter
Duke of Oldenburg
d. 1924
(2) 1916
Nicholas Kulikovsky

Olga
1895–1918

Tatiana
1897–1918

Marie
1899–1918

Anastasia
1901–1918

Alexis
1904–1918

98

81 *Left* **Alexander II, Tsar and Autocrat of All The Russias, 1870**
He reigned from 1855 to 1881, having succeeded his father Nikolai I at the close of the Crimean War. Alexander II had seven children by his marriage to Princess Marie of Hesse and by Rhine. He also had four illegitimate children by his mistress, Princess Catherine Dolgoruky, a member of an aristocratic Russian family. When the Tsarina died in 1880, Alexander hastily married the Princess in the following month. One Sunday in March of the following year, 1881, the Tsar was assassinated when an anarchist threw a bomb at his carriage.

82 *Above* **General George Custer, Grand Duke Alexis of Russia, and Buffalo Bill, 1871**
In the autumn of 1871, Grand Duke Alexis, fourth son of Tsar Alexander II, visited the United States with the Russian fleet. The Grand Duke wanted to visit the prairie and hunt buffalo, and Bill Cody was to be his guide. At the end of a five-day hunt, the Grand Duke had succeeded in bagging a total of eight buffalo. Alexis was delighted with his trip and gave Buffalo Bill a pair of diamond-studded buffalo head cufflinks and a diamond tie-pin. General George Custer was invited to accompany the party. It was also arranged that the famous Sioux Chief Spotted Tail was to appear with his warriors. Buffalo Bill was uneasy at their presence, as this Chief was one of Sitting Bull's ablest Chiefs and indeed later led his men at the Battle of Little Big Horn, which resulted in General Custer's death.

83   Alexander II, Tsar and Autocrat of All The Russias at the front with his troops, 1878
This was the third war between Russia and Turkey in the nineteenth century. In 1877, the year after the Turks had crushed Serbian resistance, Russia entered the war on behalf of its fellow Slavs. After the defeat of Turkey, Montenegro, Serbia and Rumania secured their independence, and Bulgaria became an autonomous state. Russia gained territory in Armenia. Only British political pressure stopped the Russians advancing on Constantinople.

84   *Left* Tsarevitch Nikolai, 1880
Eldest son of Tsar Alexander III, he succeeded his father in 1894. Here he is wearing the uniform of the Chevalier Guard, which was the elite Guard Regiment formed by Peter the Great in 1724. Made of white cloth with red facings, the uniform is decorated with gold lace and the metal helmet is surmounted by the Russian Eagle.

85   Grand Duke Sergei of Russia, fifth son of Tsar Alexander II

He was born in 1857, and married Elisabeth, daughter of Grand Duke Ludwig IV of Hesse and by Rhine. He was murdered in Moscow in 1905 and his wife was murdered by the Bolsheviks in 1918. He is wearing the uniform of His Majesty's Life Guard Hussar Regiment.

86 *Left* **Tsar Nikolai II of All The Russias and George, Prince of Wales at Barton Manor, Osborne, August 1909**

These two royal princes were so alike that one was often mistaken for the other. Their mothers were sisters, daughters of King Christian IX of Denmark, which may have accounted for the similarity. The journey from Russia was usually made by the Tsar and his family on their yacht the 'Standard'. Twice a year she steamed from the Baltic to the Black Sea and back again, which allowed a visit to Queen Victoria and her family at Osborne. The Imperial Family could relax for these two months, although state papers brought by messenger came constantly from St Petersburg for the Tsar's attention.

87 *Top* **The Tsar at Church Parade, 1900**

Tsar Nikolai II of All The Russias is seen here watching the regimental colours being blessed by the priests. It is summer, hence the white jackets worn by the troops. The Russian Army was vast by any standards, as from 1874 universal conscription was enforced. The infantry consisted of a hundred and ninety-two regiments, and there were some fifty-six cavalry regiments, as well as Cossacks and other irregular troops. For all this, the army was badly trained and badly commanded. The humiliating defeat in 1904 by the Japanese did not result in reforms, and the army was virtually destroyed in the First World War, which was quickly followed by revolution and civil war.

88 **The Tsar and Tsarina leaving the Winter Palace, 1905**

Tsar Nikolai II of All The Russias in the uniform of a Russian Marshal rides at the side of the Tsarina's carriage as they leave the Winter Palace at Tsarskoe Selo, thirteen miles from St Petersburg.

The new Royal House of Sweden was founded by one of Napoleon's marshals, Bernadotte. He was chosen by the Swedish Parliament and army, partly because of his humane treatment of Swedish prisoners after the Pomeranian campaign of 1807. He had also been persuaded not to invade Sweden. He ruled as Carl XIV for twenty-six years and was then succeeded by his only son Oscar I, a great diplomat.

Oscar I proposed to enter the Crimean War on the side of the Allies against Russia, but the war ended before his plans could be put into practice. His son Carl XV lost most of the royal power to Parliament during his reign. In 1872 he was succeeded by his brother Oscar II, during whose reign Norway became an independent Kingdom in 1905.

Under the influence of Emperor Wilhelm II, Prince Carl of Denmark was chosen as the new king of Norway. He took the name of Haakon VII after the Viking monarchs, and was married to an English Princess, his cousin Princess Maud, daughter of Edward VII.

Denmark's King Frederik VII had scandalised his subjects by his affairs; having twice been divorced, he had now married a former dancer, Louise Rasmussen, who had previously been his mistress. The King was also childless, and there were no male heirs to the immediate royal family. The Crown therefore devolved upon a junior branch of the royal house, Christian IX in 1863. The following year a war was fought with Prussia over the Duchies of Schleswig and Holstein. It was a complicated political affair that led to the war; as Lord Palmerston used to say, 'there are only three people who have ever understood anything about this affair: the Prince Consort, who has just died; a German professor, who went mad, and I myself, who have forgotten what it is all about'.

The King's second son became King of Greece as George I, his eldest daughter was the Princess of Wales, and the second, Dagmar, was Empress of All The Russias. His youngest daughter Thrya was married to the Crown Prince of Hanover. The King reigned on until 1906, when he was succeeded by his eldest son Frederik VII, who reigned for six years before his son became king as Christian X in 1912. King Christian's brother was elected King of Norway in 1905.

SWEDEN

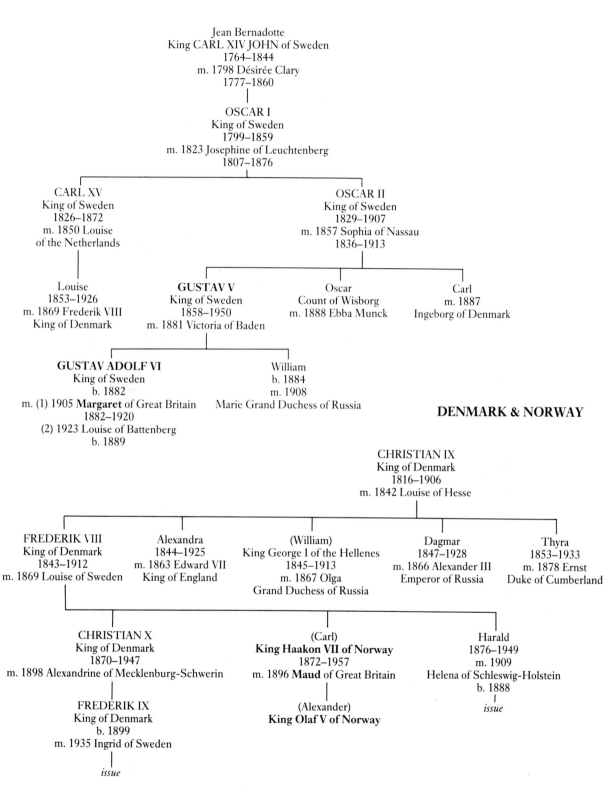

Jean Bernadotte
King CARL XIV JOHN of Sweden
1764–1844
m. 1798 Désirée Clary
1777–1860

OSCAR I
King of Sweden
1799–1859
m. 1823 Josephine of Leuchtenberg
1807–1876

CARL XV
King of Sweden
1826–1872
m. 1850 Louise
of the Netherlands

OSCAR II
King of Sweden
1829–1907
m. 1857 Sophia of Nassau
1836–1913

Louise
1853–1926
m. 1869 Frederik VIII
King of Denmark

GUSTAV V
King of Sweden
1858–1950
m. 1881 Victoria of Baden

Oscar
Count of Wisborg
m. 1888 Ebba Munck

Carl
m. 1887
Ingeborg of Denmark

GUSTAV ADOLF VI
King of Sweden
b. 1882
m. (1) 1905 **Margaret** of Great Britain
1882–1920
(2) 1923 Louise of Battenberg
b. 1889

William
b. 1884
m. 1908
Marie Grand Duchess of Russia

DENMARK & NORWAY

CHRISTIAN IX
King of Denmark
1816–1906
m. 1842 Louise of Hesse

FREDERIK VIII
King of Denmark
1843–1912
m. 1869 Louise of Sweden

Alexandra
1844–1925
m. 1863 Edward VII
King of England

(William)
King George I of the Hellenes
1845–1913
m. 1867 Olga
Grand Duchess of Russia

Dagmar
1847–1928
m. 1866 Alexander III
Emperor of Russia

Thyra
1853–1933
m. 1878 Ernst
Duke of Cumberland

CHRISTIAN X
King of Denmark
1870–1947
m. 1898 Alexandrine of Mecklenburg-Schwerin

(Carl)
King Haakon VII of Norway
1872–1957
m. 1896 **Maud** of Great Britain

Harald
1876–1949
m. 1909
Helena of Schleswig-Holstein
b. 1888

issue

FREDERIK IX
King of Denmark
b. 1899
m. 1935 Ingrid of Sweden

(Alexander)
King Olaf V of Norway

issue

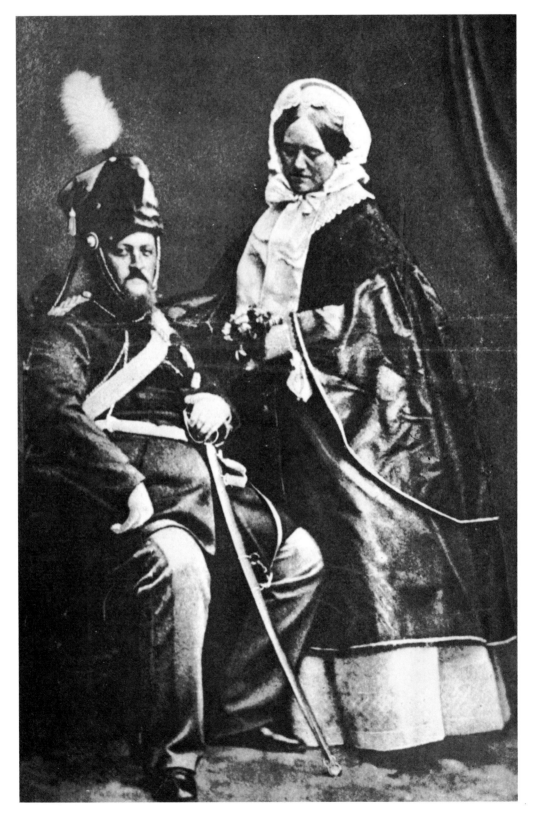

89 *Left* **Frederik VII, King of Denmark with his morganatic wife Countess Danner, 1860**
The King had already scandalised his relations by having divorced two wives, when he gave them apoplexy by living with a former dancer and milliner, Louise Rasmussen. They married in 1850, and the King gave her the title Countess Danner. Despite his marriages the King was childless and there were no immediate heirs to the Danish throne. When he died in 1863, he was succeeded by Prince Christian of Schleswig-Holstein-Sonderburg-Glucksburg, from a junior branch of the family.

90 Crown Prince Gustav of Sweden, 1880
Prince Gustav was born in 1858 and was the godchild of Queen Desirée, the wife of King Carl XIV, who had previously been Jean Baptiste Bernadotte, Marshal of France under Napoleon I. She died in 1860. Prince Gustav did not succeed his father King Oscar II until 1907. He married Princess Victoria, only daughter of Friedrich I, Grand Duke of Baden.

91 Prince Gustav Adolf of Sweden and Princess Margaret of Connaught on their wedding day, 15 June 1905
The couple were married in St George's Chapel Windsor and the honeymoon was spent in Ireland. Gustav did not succeed until 1950, as his father, King Gustav V lived to be ninety-two – and played tennis until he was eighty. His son also lived to be over ninety, and reigned for twenty-three years. Princess Margaret died in 1920, and in 1923 the Prince married Lady Louise Mountbatten, daughter of Louis, First Marquis of Milford Haven, formerly Prince of Battenberg.

92 *Right* Prince and Princess Carl of Denmark with their son Prince Alexander, 1905
In 1905 Norway became independent. Under the influence of the German Emperor Wilhelm II, a royal democratic constitution was agreed, with Prince Carl, the second son of Frederick VIII of Denmark as King. He took the name Haakon VII, after the Viking Kings, and his son's name was changed to Olav, later to succeed as Olav V. Queen Maud was the daughter of Edward VII of England. The country had no aristocracy and therefore no court life, which made the place dull compared with other European monarchies.

SPAIN AND PORTUGAL

The earliest Spanish royal photographs are those of Queen Isabella II, who had succeeded her father Fernando VII in spite of Salic law which said only the male could succeed. A volatile and amorous woman, her love affairs were as famous as they were varied. Her ministers were quite unable to persuade her to mend her ways. At the end of her life the Queen was very corpulant, which should have restrained her ardours or, at least, discouraged her suitors, but this was not the case and she continued to entertain handsome guardsmen until her death. The Queen was deposed in a coup, led by an ex-lover, Serrano, in 1868 and died in 1904. In 1870 the throne was offered to the Italian Prince Amadeo who only reigned for two years before he abdicated. A short-lived Republic followed, before the reinstatement of the monarchy in the person of Alfonso XII, Queen Isabella's son. He restored the prestige of the Royal House that had been diminished by the reign of his mother and the squabbles of his relations. He died of tuberculosis in 1885, at the early age of twenty-seven. Six months later his widow, Queen Maria Cristina, gave birth to a son, Alfonso XIII. He later married a grand-daughter of Queen Victoria, Princess Victoria Eugénie of Battenberg.

In Portugal Dom Luis succeeded his brother Pedro V, who had died of typhoid in 1861. He was stout and blond with little taste for politics, which made his reign one of stability. He was succeeded in 1889 by his son, Carlos 1, a stout and genial character, who was a great friend of Edward VII of Great Britain. The reforms imposed by his Government increased undeservedly the political unpopularity of the King; on the first of February 1908, he was assassinated together with his eldest son Luis, Duke of Braganza. His younger son, Prince Manoel, became King unexpectedly under these tragic circumstances, at the age of eighteen. He managed to retain his throne until 1910, when a naval mutiny and the threat of civil war made him decide to leave the country and settle in England, where he died in 1932.

SPAIN

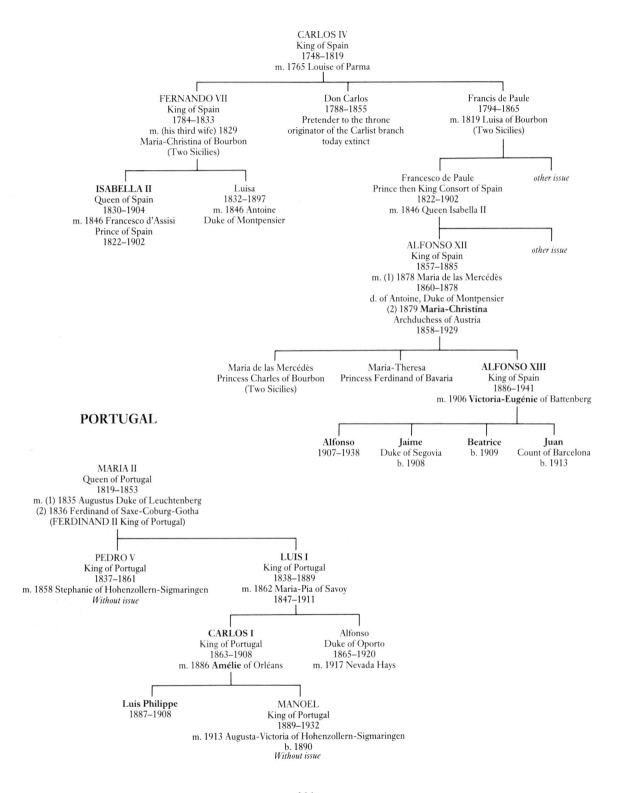

CARLOS IV
King of Spain
1748–1819
m. 1765 Louise of Parma

FERNANDO VII
King of Spain
1784–1833
m. (his third wife) 1829
Maria-Christina of Bourbon
(Two Sicilies)

Don Carlos
1788–1855
Pretender to the throne
originator of the Carlist branch
today extinct

Francis de Paule
1794–1865
m. 1819 Luisa of Bourbon
(Two Sicilies)

ISABELLA II
Queen of Spain
1830–1904
m. 1846 Francesco d'Assisi
Prince of Spain
1822–1902

Luisa
1832–1897
m. 1846 Antoine
Duke of Montpensier

Francesco de Paule
Prince then King Consort of Spain
1822–1902
m. 1846 Queen Isabella II

other issue

ALFONSO XII
King of Spain
1857–1885
m. (1) 1878 Maria de las Mercédès
1860–1878
d. of Antoine, Duke of Montpensier
(2) 1879 **Maria-Christina**
Archduchess of Austria
1858–1929

other issue

Maria de las Mercédès
Princess Charles of Bourbon
(Two Sicilies)

Maria-Theresa
Princess Ferdinand of Bavaria

ALFONSO XIII
King of Spain
1886–1941
m. 1906 **Victoria-Eugénie** of Battenberg

Alfonso
1907–1938

Jaime
Duke of Segovia
b. 1908

Beatrice
b. 1909

Juan
Count of Barcelona
b. 1913

PORTUGAL

MARIA II
Queen of Portugal
1819–1853
m. (1) 1835 Augustus Duke of Leuchtenberg
(2) 1836 Ferdinand of Saxe-Coburg-Gotha
(FERDINAND II King of Portugal)

PEDRO V
King of Portugal
1837–1861
m. 1858 Stephanie of Hohenzollern-Sigmaringen
Without issue

LUIS I
King of Portugal
1838–1889
m. 1862 Maria-Pia of Savoy
1847–1911

CARLOS I
King of Portugal
1863–1908
m. 1886 **Amélie** of Orléans

Alfonso
Duke of Oporto
1865–1920
m. 1917 Nevada Hays

Luis Philippe
1887–1908

MANOEL
King of Portugal
1889–1932
m. 1913 Augusta-Victoria of Hohenzollern-Sigmaringen
b. 1890
Without issue

93 *Left* **Queen Isabella II and Queen Maria Cristina of Spain and the Indies, with King Alfonso XIII, 1895**

When King Fernando VII died in 1833, he was succeeded by his daughter Isabella II, instead of his brother, Don Carlos. The subsequent protests of the legitimists caused the Carlist Wars, which continued sporadically throughout the nineteenth century. The new Queen was not discreet with her love affairs, since her husband, Infante Don Francesco D'Assisi, was unable to satisfy her. She once despairingly described her wedding night to one of her friends 'what do you think of a man who was wearing more lace than I was?' Throughout her reign she had a predilection for handsome guardsmen. The Queen was ousted in the coup of 1868. Her son Alfonso XII regained the throne in 1874, reigning until his death in 1885, six months before the birth of his son, Alfonso XIII, shown here with his mother the Queen Regent, Maria Cristina.

94 *Above, left* **King Amadeo I of Spain, 1870**

Prince Amadeo, First Duke of Aosta, was the second son of King Vittorio Emanuele II of Italy. When Spain deposed Queen Isabella II in 1868, the government searched for a suitable king from another Catholic dynasty, and Prince Amadeo accepted the throne. He had a strong sense of duty, but was unpopular with the Spanish, who called him 'King Macaroni'. After a reign of only two years the situation became impossible and the King abdicated. There followed an equally short-lived Republic, before the Bourbon monarchy was restored by Alfonso XII, then seventeen and a cadet at Sandhurst.

95 *Above, right* **King Alfonso XIII and Queen Victoria Eugénie of Spain and the Indies, 1906**

King Alfonso XIII was King from birth although under the regency of his mother until 1902. He was dashing, courteous and courageous, and was able to regain the people's affection for the monarchy, which had been damaged by the blunderings, quarrels and intrigues of the Royal Family. In 1906 he married Princess Victoria Eugénie, only daughter of Prince Heinrich of Battenberg and Princess Beatrice, a daughter of Queen Victoria.

96 *Left* **Queen Victoria Eugénie of Spain, 1912**
A granddaughter of Queen Victoria, the Princess
married King Alfonso XIII in 1906, and they had
seven children. Their eldest son Alfonso, Prince of
the Asturias, renounced his rights of succession so
that he could marry a divorced woman. The second
son Don Jaime was deaf and dumb, and so renounced
his rights in favour of his younger brother Don Juan,
Count of Barcelona. His eldest son Juan Carlos has
succeeded as King of Spain. The Queen is wearing
the uniform of the Cazadores Victoria Eugénie, of
which she was Colonel-in-Chief.

97 **Christening of Infanta Maria Cristina of
Spain, 1911**
On the extreme left is King Alfonso XIII. In the
centre, the Queen Mother Maria Cristina holds the
baby Princess. On the left stand the three elder sons
of the King: Prince Jaime, Duke of Segovia, Prince
Alfonso, Prince of the Asturias, and Prince Juan,
Prince of the Asturias from 1933 and head of the
Royal House of Spain after the abdication of Alfonso
XIII, in Rome in 1941.

98 *Left* **King Luis of Portugal, 1885**
'He is a good, kind amiable boy, whom one must like', wrote Queen Victoria. As King, he was a great success, despite maintaining an extravagant court, and his reign was one of prosperity and stability. He married the beautiful Princess Maria Pia of Italy, a pious lady, and they had two children, the future King Carlos and Alfonso, Duke of Oporto. The King translated *Othello, Hamlet, Richard III* and *The Merchant of Venice* into Portuguese. In the photograph, King Luis is wearing the uniform of a Portuguese Field Marshal.

99 **King Carlos I and Queen Amélie of Portugal, 1889**
A portly and genial man, the King was a great friend of Edward VII. In his leisure time he was a painter and also an excellent shot. His Queen, Amélie, was the daughter of Prince Louis Philippe of Orleans, Count of Paris, and head of the Royal House of France. In the photograph the King is wearing the uniform of the Third Light Cavalry Regiment.

**100 Funeral Hearse of King Carlos I and
Crown Prince Luis Felipe, 1908**

While driving through Lisbon, the King and Queen
and their two sons were fired upon by assassins, who
killed the King and Crown Prince. On either side of
the hearse march Gentlemen Archers of the Guard,
in eighteenth-century uniforms. Behind is the King's
charger, covered in a black pall.

The King's younger son Manoel II succeeded to
the throne at the age of eighteen. He reigned for only
two years, before revolution forced him to abdicate.
He eventually settled in England.

101   Queen Amélie of Portugal riding a bull, 1909

Queen Amélie was a shrewd woman who could see that there were signs of widespread discontent in Portugal. She therefore attempted to win the hearts of the people, and was personally very popular. Her reputation was enhanced by her rescue of a drowning fisherman, for which brave act Kaiser Wilhelm II sent her a life-saving medal. The tragic death of her husband and eldest son resulted in her younger son becoming king unexpectedly in 1908. Unrest forced the Royal Family into exile in 1910.

102 King Manoel II of Portugal and Suite, 1910
The King succeeded to the throne on the
assassination of his father and elder brother in 1908.
In October 1910 an insurrection broke out which was
supported by the navy. Mutinous ships bombarded
the Royal Palace at Lisbon and forced the King to
board his yacht for Gibraltar and, subsequently,
England. He settled in London and married Princess
Augusta Victoria of Hollenzollern-Sigmaringen in
1913. There were no children and when the King
died in 1932, the throne was claimed by Dom Duarte,
Duke of Braganza, a rival branch of the family. In the
photograph King Manoel, aged twenty-one, is
surrounded by members of his Government.